Keto Mediterranean Diet Cookbook for Beginners

Healthy Ketogenic Mediterranean Recipes with Pictures for a Balanced Lifestyle

Hunter Ramos

Author's Message

Before you start reading, I would like to thank you all and each for taking the time to read my cookbook.

It means a lot to me that out of thousands other books you've chosen mine.

In this cookbook, I tried to incorporate my experience with my knowledge and I tried my best not only to make this guide useful but also simple to read for anyone.

Each reader is my friend who is valuable to me.

TABLE OF CONTENTS

Introduction

The Keto Mediterranean Diet is a hybrid approach designed to provide the health benefits of both dietary practices while minimizing their individual drawbacks. This cookbook will guide you through this innovative diet, focusing on delicious and nutritious recipes that will transform your eating habits and improve your overall well-being.

The Keto Mediterranean Diet emphasizes a low carbohydrate intake, typically less than 50 grams per day, to promote ketosis. In ketosis, your body burns fat for energy instead of carbohydrates, leading to effective weight loss and improved metabolic health.

Whole, unprocessed foods are at the heart of this dietary approach, ensuring a rich intake of vitamins, minerals, antioxidants, and phytonutrients. The emphasis on vegetables, herbs, and spices not only enhances the nutritional profile of your meals but also brings vibrant flavors and colors to your plate.

The Keto Mediterranean Diet offers a multitude of health benefits. By promoting ketosis and providing high satiety from fat and protein, it supports effective weight loss. The Mediterranean elements of the diet contribute to improved heart health through the consumption of healthy fats and nutrient-rich foods. Additionally, the low carbohydrate intake helps stabilize blood sugar levels, making this diet particularly beneficial for individuals with insulin resistance or diabetes. The inclusion of anti-inflammatory foods further aids in reducing inflammation and preventing chronic diseases.

In this cookbook, you'll find a diverse array of recipes that embody the principles of the Keto Mediterranean Diet. From hearty breakfasts to satisfying dinners, each recipe is crafted to be both delicious and healthful. Whether you are new to this dietary approach or looking to expand your culinary repertoire, the Keto Mediterranean Cookbook will inspire you to embrace a healthier lifestyle with every meal.

The Benefits of Keto Mediterranean Diet

The Keto Mediterranean Diet merges the principles of the ketogenic and Mediterranean diets to offer a variety of health benefits while minimizing drawbacks.

By reducing carbohydrate intake to less than 50 grams per day, the diet induces ketosis, where the body burns fat for energy, leading to effective weight loss and improved metabolic health. High fat and protein intake also increase satiety, helping to reduce overall calorie consumption.

The diet emphasizes healthy fats from olive oil, avocados, nuts, seeds, and fatty fish, which improve heart health by reducing bad cholesterol (LDL) and increasing good cholesterol (HDL). The inclusion of antioxidant-rich vegetables, herbs, and spices further supports cardiovascular health.

Low carbohydrate intake helps stabilize blood sugar levels, benefiting individuals with insulin resistance or diabetes by improving insulin sensitivity and maintaining consistent blood sugar levels. Rich in anti-inflammatory foods like fatty fish, nuts, seeds, and healthy oils, the diet helps reduce inflammation and lower the risk of chronic diseases, including heart disease, diabetes, and certain cancers.

Emphasizing whole, unprocessed foods ensures a rich intake of essential vitamins, minerals, antioxidants, and phytonutrients, supporting various bodily functions, enhancing immune health, and contributing to overall well-being.

Ketosis can enhance mental performance, focus, and cognitive abilities. The diet's anti-inflammatory properties further support brain health and may reduce the risk of neurodegenerative diseases.

What to eat?

The Keto Mediterranean Diet combines the low-carb, high-fat principles of the ketogenic diet with the nutrient-rich, heart-healthy foods of the Mediterranean diet. This approach offers delicious and nutritious foods that support weight loss, heart health, and overall well-being.

Protein sources include fish and seafood like salmon, mackerel, sardines, trout, shrimp, crab, and mussels, which provide omega-3 fatty acids and lean protein. Poultry such as chicken and turkey should be skinless to maintain moderate fat content. Eggs, especially whole eggs, are rich in protein and essential nutrients, while dairy products like feta, mozzarella, goat cheese, and Greek yogurt offer protein and probiotics.

Healthy fats are crucial, with olive oil as the primary fat source, and avocado oil ideal for high-temperature cooking. Avocados, almonds, walnuts, macadamia nuts, chia seeds, flaxseeds, and sunflower seeds provide healthy fats, fiber, and essential nutrients.

Vegetables are essential, with leafy greens like spinach, kale, and arugula being low in carbs and high in vitamins. Cruciferous vegetables such as broccoli, cauliflower, and Brussels sprouts offer fiber and phytonutrients. Other vegetables like zucchini, bell peppers, and eggplant add variety and nutrients.

Low-carb fruits, particularly berries like strawberries, blueberries, and raspberries, can be consumed in small amounts for antioxidants and vitamins without significantly affecting blood sugar levels. Fresh herbs such as basil, oregano, rosemary, and thyme, and spices like turmeric, cumin, and paprika, enhance flavor and provide health benefits.

Focusing on these food groups, individuals can enjoy a variety of meals that support their health goals while adhering to the Keto Mediterranean Diet.

What to avoid?

To achieve the desired health benefits, it is essential to avoid certain foods that can hinder progress or counteract the advantages of dietary plan. High-carbohydrate foods should be avoided. This includes grains and starches such as bread, pasta, rice, and other grains, which can spike blood sugar levels and prevent the body from maintaining ketosis. Sugary foods and beverages, including snacks, desserts, candies, sodas, and fruit juices, are high in sugar and carbs and should be eliminated to support ketosis. Starchy vegetables like potatoes, sweet potatoes, and corn should be avoided due to their high carbohydrate levels, which can disrupt ketosis.

Processed and refined foods are another category to steer clear of. These foods, including processed meats, pre-packaged snacks, and convenience meals, often contain unhealthy fats, added sugars, and preservatives that can negatively impact health and disrupt the balance of a nutrient-rich diet. Unhealthy fats should also be avoided. This includes trans fats and highly processed oils, such as margarine, vegetable oils, and hydrogenated oils, which can contribute to inflammation and other health issues. High-sugar fruits should be avoided or consumed in minimal amounts. Fruits like bananas, grapes, mangoes, and cherries are high in natural sugars and can impact blood sugar levels and ketosis. Instead, opt for low-sugar fruits like berries in moderation.

Finally, alcohol and high-calorie beverages should be limited. Alcoholic drinks, especially those with added sugars or mixers, and high-calorie beverages like sweetened coffee drinks and energy drinks can add unnecessary calories and sugars, disrupting ketosis and weight loss efforts. By avoiding these high-carbohydrate, processed, and sugary foods, as well as unhealthy fats and high-sugar fruits, individuals can better adhere to the principles of the Keto Mediterranean Diet and achieve their health and wellness goals.

Tips on Keeping the Keto Mediterranean Diet

1. Incorporate olive oil, avocado oil, and coconut oil as your primary cooking fats. These healthy fats not only add flavor but also support ketosis.

2. Plan your weekly meals in advance to ensure you stay within your carb limits and have all necessary ingredients on hand. This helps avoid last-minute temptations.

3. Keep your pantry and fridge stocked with keto Mediterranean staples like olive oil, avocados, nuts, seeds, fatty fish, cheese, and low-carb vegetables.

4. Drink plenty of water throughout the day. Staying hydrated helps manage hunger and supports overall health.

5. Use a food diary or a mobile app to track your carbohydrate, protein, and fat intake. This ensures you stay within your daily limits and maintain ketosis.

6. Consider intermittent fasting to enhance ketosis and weight loss. For example, follow a 16:8 fasting schedule where you fast for 16 hours and eat during an 8-hour window.

7. Keep your meals interesting by trying new keto Mediterranean recipes. This prevents boredom and helps you discover new favorite dishes.

8. Even healthy foods can lead to weight gain if eaten in large quantities. Be mindful of portion sizes, especially with high-calorie foods like nuts and cheese.

9. Carefully read food labels to avoid hidden sugars and carbs in packaged foods. Opt for whole, unprocessed foods whenever possible.

10. Plan for social events by eating a small meal beforehand, bringing a keto-friendly dish, or choosing Mediterranean options that fit your diet, such as grilled meats and salads.

11. Since the keto diet can lead to a loss of electrolytes, make sure to include foods rich in potassium, magnesium, and sodium. Leafy greens, nuts, seeds, avocados, and bone broth are excellent sources.

12. Plan for social events by eating a small meal beforehand, bringing a keto-friendly dish, or choosing Mediterranean options that fit your diet, such as grilled meats and salads.

BREAKFASTS

INGREDIENTS

- 4 slices keto bread, 2 ripe avocados
- 1 small red onion, finely chopped
- 10 cherry tomatoes, halved
- 1/4 cup crumbled feta cheese
- 2 tablespoons olive oil
- 1 tbsp lemon juice, 1/4 tsp salt
- 1/4 teaspoon black pepper, fresh dill
- 1 clove garlic, peeled

Aegean Avocado Toast on Keto Bread

 15 mins   5 min   4

O1 Toast the keto bread slices until golden and crispy. In a bowl, mash the avocados with the lemon juice, salt, and pepper. Rub each slice of toast with the garlic clove, then spread the mashed avocado evenly over each slice.

O2 Top each slice with red onion, cherry tomatoes, and crumbled feta cheese. Drizzle olive oil over each piece of toast and garnish with fresh dill.

O3 Serve immediately.

NUTRITIONAL VALUE

290 calories, 7g protein, 12g carbohydrates, 23g fat, 7g fiber, 15mg cholesterol, 320mg sodium, 510mg potassium.

INGREDIENTS

- 2 cups fullfat Greek yogurt
- 1/2 cup chopped walnuts, toasted
- 2 tablespoons monk fruit sweetener
- 1/2 teaspoon ground cinnamon
- 1/4 teaspoon vanilla extract
- 2 tablespoons ground flaxseed

Greek Yogurt & Walnut Parfait with Cinnamon

 10 mins   0 min   4

O1 In a medium bowl, mix Greek yogurt with monk fruit sweetener, cinnamon, and vanilla extract until well combined. In serving glasses, layer half of the yogurt mixture, followed by a layer of chopped walnuts and a sprinkle of ground flaxseed.

O2 Repeat the layers with the remaining ingredients, finishing with a layer of walnuts and a sprinkle of cinnamon on top for garnish.

O3 Chill in the refrigerator for at least 30 minutes before serving to allow the flavors to meld.

NUTRITIONAL VALUE

230 calories, 12g protein, 8g carbohydrates, 18g fat, 3g fiber, 30mg cholesterol, 45mg sodium, 200mg potassium.

Mediterranean Frittata with Spinach and Feta

🕐 10 mins   🍲 20 min   👤 4

INGREDIENTS

- 8 large eggs
- 1 cup fresh spinach, chopped
- 1/2 cup feta cheese, crumbled
- 1/4 cup heavy cream
- 1 small red onion, finely diced·
- 2 cloves garlic, minced
- 2 tablespoons olive oil
- 1/2 tsp salt, 1/4 tsp black pepper
- 1/4 teaspoon dried oregano

01 Preheat the oven to 375°F (190°C). Sauté the onion and garlic in olive oil until translucent, about 3-4 minutes. Add the spinach and cook until wilted, about 2 minutes.

02 Whisk together the eggs, heavy cream, salt, pepper, and oregano in a large bowl. Stir in the sautéed vegetables and feta cheese. Pour the mixture into a greased 9-inch pie dish or cast iron skillet.

03 Bake for 18-20 minutes or until the eggs are set and golden. Remove from the oven, let cool slightly, and serve.

NUTRITIONAL VALUE

295 calories, 18g protein, 4g carbohydrates, 23g fat, 1g fiber, 390mg cholesterol, 590mg sodium, 280mg potassium.

Poached Eggs with Yogurt and Spiced Butter

🕐 10 mins   🍲 10 min   👤 4

INGREDIENTS

- 8 large eggs, 1 cup full-fat Greek yogurt, 2 cloves garlic, minced
- 4 tablespoons unsalted butter
- 1 teaspoon paprika
- 1/2 teaspoon red pepper flakes
- 2 tablespoons white vinegar
- Salt and black pepper, to taste
- Fresh dill, chopped, for garnish

01 Mix Greek yogurt with minced garlic and a pinch of salt. Spread the mixture on four plates as a base.

02 Simmer water with vinegar in a saucepan. Poach the eggs for 3-4 minutes. Remove with a slotted spoon and drain.

03 Melt butter, add paprika and red pepper flakes. Place two poached eggs on each plate over the yogurt, drizzle with spiced butter, sprinkle with dill, and season. Serve immediately.

NUTRITIONAL VALUE

330 calories, 19g protein, 5g carbohydrates, 27g fat, 0g fiber, 425mg cholesterol, 320mg sodium, 230mg potassium.

INGREDIENTS

- 6 large eggs, 2 large bell peppers, sliced, 1 medium onion, sliced
- 2 cloves garlic, minced
- 1 can (14 oz) diced tomatoes, no sugar added, 2 tablespoons olive oil
- 1 tsp cumin, 1/2 tsp paprika
- 1/4 teaspoon chili powder
- Salt and black pepper, to taste
- Fresh parsley, chopped, for garnish

LowCarb Shakshuka with Bell Peppers

 10 mins   20 min   4

01 Heat olive oil in a large skillet over medium heat. Add sliced onions and bell peppers, cooking until softened, about 5 minutes. Add garlic and cook for another minute.

02 Stir in diced tomatoes, cumin, paprika, chili powder, salt, and black pepper. Simmer for 10 minutes until the mixture thickens slightly.

03 Make six wells in the tomato mixture and crack an egg into each well. Cover and cook until egg whites are set but yolks are runny, about 8-10 minutes. Garnish with chopped parsley before serving.

NUTRITIONAL VALUE	215 calories, 13g protein, 10g carbohydrates, 14g fat, 3g fiber, 372mg cholesterol, 320mg sodium, 450mg potassium.

INGREDIENTS

- 1 cup almond flour, 1/2 cup ricotta cheese, 2 large eggs
- 1/4 cup unsweetened almond milk
- 2 tablespoons granulated erythritol
- 1 lemon (zest and juice), 1 tsp baking powder, 1/2 tsp vanilla extract
- Butter or coconut oil, for cooking
- Fresh berries and sugarfree syrup

Sicilian Lemon Ricotta Pancakes

 15 mins   10 min   4

01 In a large bowl, combine almond flour, ricotta cheese, eggs, almond milk, erythritol, lemon zest, lemon juice, baking powder, and vanilla extract. Whisk until smooth.

02 Heat a nonstick skillet over medium heat and add butter or coconut oil. Pour about 1/4 cup of batter for each pancake into the skillet. Cook for 2-3 minutes on each side until golden brown.

03 Serve the pancakes warm with optional fresh berries and sugar-free syrup.

NUTRITIONAL VALUE	90 calories, 7g protein, 2g carbohydrates, 6g fat, 1g fiber, 185mg cholesterol, 125mg sodium, 125mg potassium.

Catalan Spinach and Chorizo Omelette

 10 mins   15 min   4

01 In a large bowl, whisk eggs with salt and black pepper. Stir in chopped spinach, diced chorizo, and red bell pepper.

02 Heat olive oil in a large nonstick skillet over medium heat. Pour the egg mixture into the skillet, spreading the fillings evenly.

03 Cook for about 7-8 minutes until edges lift from the pan. Sprinkle grated Manchego cheese over the top, fold the omelette in half, and cook for another 2 minutes until the cheese is melted. Slide the omelette onto a plate, cut into servings, and serve warm.

INGREDIENTS

- 8 large eggs
- 1/2 cup cooked chorizo, diced
- 1 cup fresh spinach, roughly chopped
- 1/4 cup grated Manchego cheese
- 1/4 cup red bell pepper, diced
- 2 tablespoons olive oil
- Salt and black pepper, to taste

NUTRITIONAL VALUE

320 calories, 21g protein, 3g carbohydrates, 25g fat, 1g fiber, 390mg cholesterol, 620mg sodium, 300mg potassium.

Keto Tzatziki Cucumber Boats

 20 mins   0 min   6

01 Cut the cucumbers in half lengthwise and scoop out the seeds to create a hollow boat.

02 In a bowl, combine Greek yogurt, garlic, dill, olive oil, and lemon juice. Season with salt and pepper and mix until smooth.

03 Fill the cucumber boats with the yogurt mixture. Top with diced red onion and sliced kalamata olives. Chill for 15 minutes before serving to allow the flavors to meld.

INGREDIENTS

- 3 large cucumbers
- 1 cup full-fat Greek yogurt
- 1 small garlic clove, minced
- 1 tablespoon fresh dill, chopped
- 1 tbsp olive oil, 1 tbsp lemon juice
- Salt and black pepper, to taste
- 1/4 cup red onion, finely diced
- 1/4 cup kalamata olives, sliced

NUTRITIONAL VALUE

85 calories, 4g protein, 5g carbohydrates, 6g fat, 1g fiber, 5mg cholesterol, 115mg sodium, 250mg potassium.

INGREDIENTS

- 12 large eggs
- 1 can (14 oz) artichoke hearts, drained and chopped
- 2 cups fresh spinach, chopped
- 1/2 cup grated Parmesan cheese
- 1/4 cup heavy cream
- 2 tbsp olive oil, salt and pepper
- Nonstick cooking spray

Florentine Artichoke and Egg Cups

 15 mins 20 min 6

O1 Preheat the oven to 375°F (190°C) and grease a 12-cup muffin tin. Heat olive oil in a skillet over medium heat, add spinach, and cook until wilted, about 2-3 minutes. Remove from heat and mix in chopped artichoke hearts.

O2 In a bowl, whisk eggs, heavy cream, Parmesan cheese, salt, and black pepper. Stir in the spinach and artichoke mixture. Divide the mixture evenly among the muffin cups, filling each about three-quarters full.

O3 Bake for 15-20 minutes until the eggs are set and tops are golden.

NUTRITIONAL VALUE 210 calories, 14g protein, 4g carbohydrates, 15g fat, 1g fiber, 372mg cholesterol, 320mg sodium, 240mg potassium.

INGREDIENTS

- 1 lb mixed mushrooms, sliced
- 1 medium red onion, thinly sliced
- 3 cloves garlic, minced
- 1/4 cup fresh parsley, chopped, 1/4 cup fresh thyme leaves
- 1/4 cup fresh rosemary, chopped
- 1/4 cup olive oil, salt and pepper
- 1/2 cup grated Gruyère cheese

Provençal Mushroom and Herb Bake

 15 mins 25 min 4

O1 Preheat oven to 375°F (190°C). Toss mushrooms, red onion, and garlic with olive oil, parsley, thyme, rosemary, salt, and pepper in a bowl.

O2 Spread the mixture in a baking dish. Cover with foil and bake for 20 minutes. Remove foil, sprinkle Gruyère cheese on top, and bake uncovered for 5 more minutes until melted and golden.

O3 Let sit for a couple of minutes before serving. Garnish with fresh herbs if desired.

NUTRITIONAL VALUE 260 calories, 10g protein, 11g carbohydrates, 20g fat, 3g fiber, 25mg cholesterol, 180mg sodium, 500mg potassium.

Caprese Omelet with Mozzarella and Basil

🕐 5 mins   🍲 10 min   👤 4

O1   Beat the eggs with salt and black pepper in a bowl.

O2   Heat olive oil in a nonstick skillet over medium heat. Pour in half the eggs and cook for 2-3 minutes until edges set. Lay half the mozzarella, tomato slices, and basil on one half of the omelet. Fold the other half over and cook for another 2 minutes until the mozzarella melts.

O3   Slide the omelet onto a plate and drizzle with balsamic vinegar reduction if desired. Repeat with remaining ingredients for a second omelet. Serve immediately.

INGREDIENTS

- 8 large eggs
- 1/2 cup fresh mozzarella, sliced
- 1 large tomato, sliced
- 1/4 cup fresh basil leaves, torn
- 2 tablespoons olive oil
- Salt and black pepper, to taste
- Optional: drizzle of balsamic vinegar reduction

NUTRITIONAL VALUE

295 calories, 21g protein, 3g carbohydrates, 23g fat, 1g fiber, 430mg cholesterol, 320mg sodium, 300mg potassium.

Savory Olive and Tomato Galette

🕐 20 mins   🍲 25 min   👤 4

O1   Combine almond flour, coconut flour, xanthan gum, and salt in a food processor. Add cold butter and pulse until coarse crumbs form. Add the egg, pulse until dough forms, wrap, and chill for 10 minutes.

O2   Preheat oven to 375°F (190°C). Roll out dough between parchment into a 12-inch circle. Transfer to a baking sheet. Toss tomatoes and olives with olive oil and thyme. Arrange on dough, leaving a 2-inch border, and sprinkle with feta.

O3   Fold edges over filling and bake for 25 minutes until crust is golden. Let cool slightly before serving.

INGREDIENTS

- 1 1/2 cups almond flour
- 1/4 cup coconut flour
- 1/2 tsp xanthan gum, 1/4 tsp salt
- 6 tablespoons cold butter, diced
- 1 large egg, 1 tbsp olive oil
- 1/2 cup cherry tomatoes, halved
- 1/4 cup black olives, pitted and sliced, 1/4 cup green olives, pitted and sliced, 1 tbsp fresh thyme leaves
- 1/4 cup crumbled feta cheese

NUTRITIONAL VALUE

380 calories, 12g protein, 14g carbohydrates, 32g fat, 7g fiber, 85mg cholesterol, 430mg sodium, 300mg potassium.

15

INGREDIENTS

- 8 ounces halloumi cheese, sliced
- 1 pound asparagus, trimmed and cut into 2inch pieces
- 2 tablespoons olive oil
- 1 teaspoon lemon zest
- 2 tablespoons lemon juice
- 1/4 cup pine nuts
- Salt and black pepper, to taste
- Fresh mint leaves, for garnish

Halloumi and Asparagus Keto Skillet

 10 mins 15 min 4

O1 Heat olive oil in a large skillet over medium-high heat. Fry halloumi slices until golden brown on both sides, about 2-3 minutes per side. Remove and set aside.

O2 In the same skillet, sauté asparagus for 5-7 minutes until tender and slightly charred. Return halloumi to the skillet.

O3 Add lemon zest, lemon juice, and pine nuts. Toss to combine and heat through. Season with salt and black pepper. Remove from heat, garnish with fresh mint leaves, and serve immediately.

NUTRITIONAL VALUE	330 calories, 18g protein, 8g carbohydrates, 26g fat, 3g fiber, 0mg cholesterol, 670mg sodium, 300mg potassium.

INGREDIENTS

- 1 pound Italian sausage, casings removed, 2 bell peppers, sliced
- 1 medium onion, sliced
- 2 cloves garlic, minced
- 2 tbsp olive oil, 1/2 tsp crushed red pepper flakes, salt and pepper
- 1/4 cup fresh basil, chopped
- Optional: grated Parmesan cheese, for serving

Italian Sausage and Pepper Hash

10 15 mins 20 min 4

O1 Heat olive oil in a skillet over medium heat. Cook Italian sausage, breaking it into pieces, until browned, about 10 minutes. Remove and set aside.

O2 In the same skillet, cook bell peppers, onion, and garlic until softened, about 10 minutes. Return sausage to the skillet.

O3 Add red pepper flakes, salt, and black pepper. Stir and cook for 2 minutes. Remove from heat, stir in basil, and serve hot. Optionally, sprinkle with Parmesan cheese.

NUTRITIONAL VALUE	410 calories, 23g protein, 9g carbohydrates, 31g fat, 2g fiber, 85mg cholesterol, 790mg sodium, 450mg potassium.

Moroccan Spiced Keto Porridge

 5 mins   10 min   4

01 In a medium saucepan, combine almond flour, coconut flour, and unsweetened almond milk. Stir over medium heat until it starts to simmer.

02 Reduce heat to low and add cinnamon, nutmeg, ginger, cloves, and erythritol. Stir continuously for 5-7 minutes until the porridge thickens.

03 Remove from heat and let sit for a couple of minutes to thicken further. Serve hot, garnished with slivered almonds and chopped dried apricots.

INGREDIENTS

- 1 cup almond flour, 2 tbsp coconut flour
- 2 cups unsweetened almond milk
- 1 tsp cinnamon, 1/2 tsp nutmeg
- 1/4 tsp ginger, 1/4 tsp cloves
- 1 tbsp erythritol or another keto-friendly sweetener, 2 tbsp slivered almonds, for garnish, 2 tbsp chopped dried apricots (sugarfree), for garnish

NUTRITIONAL VALUE

230 calories, 8g protein, 12g carbohydrates, 18g fat, 6g fiber, 0mg cholesterol, 120mg sodium, 300mg potassium.

Cypriot Egg and Avocado Bowl

 10 mins   10 min   4

01 Bring a pot of water to a boil. Add eggs and boil for 10 minutes. Transfer to ice water to cool, then peel and slice.

02 In a large bowl, combine diced avocados, cherry tomatoes, and red onion. In a small bowl, whisk lemon juice, olive oil, salt, and pepper. Pour dressing over avocado mixture and toss gently.

03 Divide avocado mixture among four bowls. Top each with sliced eggs and sprinkle with fresh parsley. Serve immediately.

INGREDIENTS

- 4 large eggs
- 2 ripe avocados, diced
- 1 cup cherry tomatoes, halved
- 1/4 cup red onion, finely chopped
- 2 tablespoons fresh lemon juice
- 2 tablespoons extra virgin olive oil
- 2 tbsp fresh parsley, chopped
- Salt and pepper, to taste

NUTRITIONAL VALUE

310 calories, 9g protein, 12g carbohydrates, 27g fat, 7g fiber, 190mg cholesterol, 150mg sodium, 650mg potassium.

INGREDIENTS

- I cup unsweetened almond milk
- I/2 cup unsweetened Greek yogurt
- I/4 cup almond butter
- I medium orange, peeled and segmented, I tbsp orange zest
- 2 tablespoons erythritol or another keto-friendly sweetener
- I/2 teaspoon vanilla extract
- I cup ice cubes

Andalusian Almond and Orange Smoothie

 10 mins 0 min 👤 4

O1 In a blender, combine almond milk, Greek yogurt, almond butter, orange segments, orange zest, erythritol, and vanilla extract.

O2 Blend on high until smooth and creamy. Add ice cubes and blend again until frothy.

O3 Pour into glasses and serve immediately.

NUTRITIONAL VALUE	180 calories, 7g protein, 10g carbohydrates, 13g fat, 3g fiber, 5mg cholesterol, 90mg sodium, 270mg potassium.

INGREDIENTS

- 2 cups full-fat Greek yogurt
- 2 tablespoons olive oil
- 2 tablespoons za'atar spice blend
- I/2 teaspoon salt
- Fresh mint leaves, for garnish
- Sliced cucumber and bell pepper, for serving

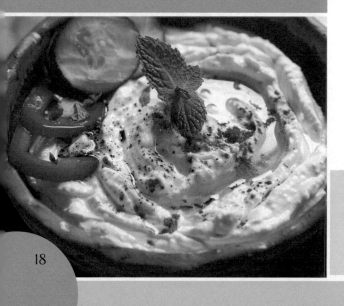

Lebanese Labneh Cheese and Za'atar Spread

 10 mins 0 min 👤 4

O1 Place Greek yogurt in a cheesecloth or fine strainer over a bowl. Let it drain in the refrigerator for at least 2 hours or overnight to thicken.

O2 Transfer the thickened yogurt (labneh) to a serving bowl. Stir in salt and half of the olive oil.

O3 Spread the labneh in the bowl, create a well in the center, drizzle with remaining olive oil, and sprinkle with za'atar. Garnish with fresh mint leaves and serve with sliced cucumber and bell pepper.

NUTRITIONAL VALUE	160 calories, 7g protein, 6g carbohydrates, 12g fat, 1g fiber, 5mg cholesterol, 300mg sodium, 250mg potassium.

SEAFOOD SPECIALTIES

INGREDIENTS

- 1 pound sea scallops, patted dry
- 3 tbsp unsalted butter, 2 tbsp olive oil
- 2 cloves garlic, minced
- Juice and zest of 1 lemon
- 1/4 cup fresh parsley, chopped
- Salt and black pepper, to taste

Amalfi Lemon Butter Scallops

 10 mins   10 min 👩‍🍳 4

O1 Heat olive oil and 1 tablespoon of butter in a skillet over medium-high heat. Season scallops with salt and black pepper.

O2 Cook scallops in a single layer for 2-3 minutes per side until golden brown and opaque. Remove and set aside.

O3 In the same skillet, add remaining butter and garlic. Cook for 1 minute until fragrant. Add lemon juice and zest, stirring to combine. Return scallops to the skillet and toss in the lemon butter sauce. Sprinkle with fresh parsley and serve immediately.

NUTRITIONAL VALUE

250 calories, 23g protein, 3g carbohydrates, 17g fat, 0g fiber, 85mg cholesterol, 370mg sodium, 350mg potassium.

INGREDIENTS

- 1 cup cauliflower rice
- 1/2 lb shrimp, peeled and deveined
- 1/2 lb mussels, cleaned, 1/2 lb calamari, sliced, 1/4 cup dry white wine
- 1 onion, chopped, 2 tbsp olive oil
- 2 cloves garlic, minced
- 2 cups chicken or seafood broth
- 1/4 cup heavy cream, salt and pepper
- 2 tablespoons fresh parsley, chopped
- Lemon wedges, for serving

Adriatic Seafood Risotto

 15 mins   30 min 👩‍🍳 4

O1 Heat olive oil in a pan over medium heat. Sauté onion and garlic until translucent.

O2 Add shrimp, mussels, and calamari. Cook until shrimp turns pink and mussels open. Pour in white wine and cook for 2 minutes until reduced. Add cauliflower rice and broth, stirring until tender and liquid is mostly absorbed.

O3 Stir in heavy cream, salt, and pepper. Cook for 2 minutes until creamy. Serve with parsley and lemon wedges.

NUTRITIONAL VALUE

320 calories, 28g protein, 7g carbohydrates, 20g fat, 2g fiber, 150mg cholesterol, 820mg sodium, 600mg potassium.

Octopus Salad with Olive Oil and Lemon

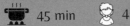 15 mins 45 min 4

INGREDIENTS

- 1 1/2 pounds octopus, cleaned
- 1/4 cup extra virgin olive oil
- Juice of 2 lemons
- 2 cloves garlic, minced
- 1/4 cup fresh parsley, chopped
- 1/4 cup red onion, thinly sliced
- 1/4 cup Kalamata olives, sliced
- 1 teaspoon dried oregano
- Salt and black pepper, to taste

O1 In a large pot, bring water to a boil. Cook the octopus for 40-45 minutes until tender. Remove, let cool, and cut into bite-sized pieces.

O2 In a large bowl, whisk together olive oil, lemon juice, minced garlic, oregano, salt, and black pepper.

O3 Add octopus, parsley, red onion, and Kalamata olives to the bowl. Toss to combine and coat evenly with the dressing. Cover and refrigerate for at least 30 minutes. Serve chilled or at room temperature.

NUTRITIONAL VALUE

220 calories, 24g protein, 4g carbohydrates, 12g fat, 1g fiber, 75mg cholesterol, 320mg sodium, 450mg potassium.

Catalan Shrimp with Garlic and Parsley

 10 mins 10 min 4

INGREDIENTS

- 1 1/2 pounds large shrimp, peeled and deveined, 1/4 cup extra virgin olive oil, 6 cloves garlic, thinly sliced, juice of 1 lemon
- 1/4 cup fresh parsley, chopped
- Salt and black pepper, to taste
- 1/2 teaspoon red pepper flakes

O1 In a large skillet, heat olive oil over medium heat. Add garlic and red pepper flakes, sauté until fragrant and golden, about 2 minutes.

O2 Add shrimp and cook, stirring frequently, until pink and opaque, about 3-4 minutes.

O3 Remove from heat and stir in lemon juice, chopped parsley, salt, and black pepper. Serve immediately, garnished with additional parsley if desired.

NUTRITIONAL VALUE

250 calories, 24g protein, 2g carbohydrates, 16g fat, 1g fiber, 220mg cholesterol, 380mg sodium, 300mg potassium.

INGREDIENTS

- 2 pounds mussels, cleaned and debearded, 2 tbsp olive oil
- 4 cloves garlic, minced
- 1 small red chili, thinly sliced
- 1 can (14.5 oz) diced tomatoes
- 1/2 cup dry white wine
- 1/4 cup fresh parsley, chopped
- Salt and black pepper, to taste

Venetian Spicy Mussels in Tomato Broth

 10 mins   15 min   4

O1 In a large pot, heat olive oil over medium heat. Add garlic and red chili, sautéing until fragrant, about 2 minutes.

O2 Pour in white wine and bring to a simmer. Add diced tomatoes, salt, and black pepper. Cook for 5 minutes to meld flavors.

O3 Add mussels, cover, and cook for 5-7 minutes until mussels open. Discard any that do not open. Stir in fresh parsley and serve immediately.

NUTRITIONAL VALUE	180 calories, 18g protein, 8g carbohydrates, 7g fat, 2g fiber, 45mg cholesterol, 540mg sodium, 500mg potassium.

INGREDIENTS

- 1 lb sea bass fillets, 1/2 lb shrimp, peeled and deveined, 1/2 lb mussels, cleaned and debearded
- 2 tbsp olive oil, 1 small fennel bulb, thinly sliced, 1 medium onion, chopped, 3 cloves garlic, minced
- 1 can diced tomatoes, 4 cups fish stock, 1/4 tsp saffron threads, 1/2 tsp smoked paprika, 1/4 tsp cayenne pepper, salt and pepper
- 1/4 cup fresh parsley, chopped

Keto Bouillabaisse with Saffron and Sea Bass

 15 mins   30 min   4

O1 Heat olive oil in a large pot over medium heat. Add fennel, onion, and garlic, sautéing until softened, about 5 minutes. Add tomatoes, fish stock, saffron, paprika, and cayenne pepper. Simmer for 10 minutes.

O2 Add sea bass, shrimp, and mussels. Cover and cook for 7-10 minutes until seafood is cooked and mussels open. Discard any unopened mussels.

O3 Stir in parsley and season with salt and black pepper. Serve hot.

NUTRITIONAL VALUE	280 calories, 30g protein, 10g carbohydrates, 12g fat, 2g fiber, 110mg cholesterol, 750mg sodium, 850mg potassium.

Iberian Clam and Chorizo Stew

🕐 15 mins   🍲 25 min   👨 4

O1 Heat olive oil in a large pan over medium heat. Add chorizo and cook until browned. Add onion, garlic, and red bell pepper, and sauté until soft.

O2 Stir in crushed tomatoes, white wine, chicken broth, and smoked paprika. Bring to a simmer. Add clams, cover, and cook for 8-10 minutes until clams open. Discard any that don't open. Season with salt and pepper.

O3 Serve hot, garnished with fresh parsley.

NUTRITIONAL VALUE

320 calories, 20g protein, 10g carbohydrates, 22g fat, 2g fiber, 70mg cholesterol, 900mg sodium, 700mg potassium.

INGREDIENTS

- 1 pound clams, cleaned
- 1/2 pound chorizo, sliced
- 1 onion, chopped, salt and pepper
- 2 cloves garlic, minced
- 1 red bell pepper, diced
- 1 cup crushed tomatoes, 1/2 cup dry white wine, 1 cup chicken broth, 2 tbsp olive oil, 1 tsp smoked paprika, fresh parsley, chopped, for garnish

Sicilian Swordfish Steaks with Caponata

🕐 15 mins   🍲 30 min   👨 4

O1 Heat 2 tablespoons of olive oil in a skillet over medium heat. Sauté eggplant, onion, garlic, bell pepper, and celery for 10 minutes.

O2 Add capers, olives, tomatoes, vinegar, and oregano. Season with salt and pepper. Simmer for 15 minutes until thickened.

O3 Heat remaining olive oil in a grill pan over medium-high heat. Season swordfish with salt and pepper. Grill for 4-5 minutes per side until cooked through. Serve with caponata and garnish with basil.

NUTRITIONAL VALUE

420 calories, 38g protein, 12g carbohydrates, 24g fat, 5g fiber, 80mg cholesterol, 600mg sodium, 800mg potassium.

INGREDIENTS

- 4 swordfish steaks, 1/4 cup olive oil, divided, 1 eggplant, diced
- 1 small onion, chopped, salt, pepper
- 2 cloves garlic, minced, 1 bell pepper, diced, 2 celery stalks, chopped, 1/4 cup capers, drained
- 1/4 cup green olives, sliced, 1 can diced tomatoes, 2 tbsp red wine vinegar, 1 tsp dried oregano
- Fresh basil leaves, for garnish

INGREDIENTS

- 1 medium eggplant, diced
- 2 tbsp olive oil
- 1 pound fresh tuna steak, finely diced
- 1 small red onion, finely chopped
- 1/4 cup capers, drained and chopped
- 1/4 cup fresh parsley, chopped
- 2 tbsp lemon juice, 1 tbsp Dijon mustard, 1 tbsp fresh thyme leaves
- Salt and black pepper, to taste

Provence Tuna and Eggplant Tartare

 15 mins 10 min   4

O1 Heat olive oil in a skillet over medium heat. Cook diced eggplant until tender and golden, about 10 minutes. Remove from heat and let cool.

O2 In a large bowl, combine diced tuna, cooled eggplant, red onion, capers, parsley, lemon juice, Dijon mustard, and thyme. Mix gently. Season with salt and black pepper to taste.

O3 Divide the tartare among four plates, shaping it into rounds if desired. Serve immediately, garnished with fresh parsley or thyme.

NUTRITIONAL VALUE

290 calories, 28g protein, 10g carbohydrates, 16g fat, 5g fiber, 50mg cholesterol, 400mg sodium, 650mg potassium.

INGREDIENTS

- 1 pound large prawns, peeled
- 8 oz halloumi cheese, cut into cubes
- 1 red bell pepper, cut into squares
- 1 yellow bell pepper, cut into squares
- 1/4 cup olive oil, 2 tbsp lemon juice
- 2 cloves garlic, minced
- 1 tsp dried oregano, salt and pepper
- Fresh parsley, chopped, for garnish

Cypriot Halloumi and Prawn Skewers

 15 mins 10 min 4

O1 In a bowl, whisk olive oil, lemon juice, garlic, oregano, salt, and black pepper. Add prawns and halloumi cubes, tossing to coat. Marinate for 10 minutes.

O2 Preheat grill to medium-high heat. Thread prawns, halloumi, and bell pepper squares onto skewers, alternating them.

O3 Grill skewers for 3-4 minutes per side until prawns are opaque and halloumi is golden brown. Remove from grill, garnish with fresh parsley, and serve immediately.

NUTRITIONAL VALUE

320 calories, 25g protein, 5g carbohydrates, 22g fat, 1g fiber, 120mg cholesterol, 520mg sodium, 300mg potassium.

Moroccan Spiced Cod with Chermoula

 15 mins   15 min   4

INGREDIENTS

- 4 cod fillets, 2 tbsp olive oil
- 1 tsp cumin, coriander, paprika
- 1/2 tsp turmeric, 1/4 tsp cayenne pepper, salt and pepper
- For the Chermoula: 1 cup cilantro, 1 cup fresh parsley, chopped, 3 cloves garlic, minced, 1 tsp cumin, coriander, 1/2 tsp paprika, Juice of 1 lemon, 1/4 cup olive oil, salt and pepper

01 Preheat oven to 400°F (200°C). Mix spices and rub on cod. Heat olive oil in a skillet, sear cod for 2-3 minutes per side. Bake for 10-12 minutes.

02 Combine cilantro, parsley, garlic, cumin, coriander, paprika, lemon juice, olive oil, salt, and pepper in a food processor. Pulse until chunky.

03 Serve baked cod topped with chermoula.

NUTRITIONAL VALUE

280 calories, 30g protein, 3g carbohydrates, 16g fat, 1g fiber, 75mg cholesterol, 300mg sodium, 700mg potassium.

Sea Bream with Oregano and Lemon Butter

 10 mins   20 min   4

INGREDIENTS

- 2 whole sea bream, cleaned and gutted,2 tbsp unsalted butter
- 2 tbsp fresh lemon juice, 2 cloves garlic, minced, salt and pepper
- 1 tbsp fresh oregano, chopped
- Lemon wedges, for serving

01 Preheat oven to 375°F (190°C) and line a baking sheet with parchment paper. Rinse and pat dry sea bream, then place on the sheet.

02 Melt butter in a saucepan over medium heat. Stir in lemon juice, garlic, and oregano for 1-2 minutes until fragrant. Brush fish with the mixture and season with salt and pepper.

03 Bake for 15-20 minutes until fish is cooked through. Serve hot, garnished with lemon wedges.

NUTRITIONAL VALUE

220 calories, 28g protein, 2g carbohydrates, 10g fat, 1g fiber, 75mg cholesterol, 180mg sodium, 450mg potassium.

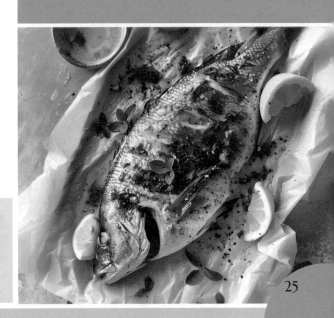

INGREDIENTS

- 1 lb (450g) mixed seafood
- 2 tbsp olive oil, 1 large onion, finely chopped, 2 cloves garlic, minced
- 2 bell peppers, chopped
- 1 large tomato, chopped
- 1 tsp paprika, cumin, oregano
- 1/2 tsp ground black pepper
- Salt, to taste, 1/2 cup fresh parsley, chopped, lemon wedges, for serving

Turkish Seafood Güveç (Clay Pot Stew)

 15 mins   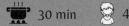 30 min   4

O1   Preheat oven to 375°F (190°C).

O2   Sauté onion and garlic in olive oil for 5 minutes in an oven-safe dish. Add bell peppers, cook 5 minutes. Stir in tomato, paprika, cumin, oregano, pepper, and salt.

O3   Add seafood, stir to coat. Cover and bake for 20-25 minutes until seafood is cooked. Garnish with parsley and serve with lemon wedges.

NUTRITIONAL VALUE	250 calories, 30g protein, 6g carbohydrates, 10g fat, 2g fiber, 150mg cholesterol, 400mg sodium, 500mg potassium.

INGREDIENTS

- 1 lb mixed seafood, 2 tbsp olive oil
- 1 medium fennel bulb, thinly sliced
- 1 small onion, chopped
- 2 cloves garlic, minced, 4 cups fish stock, 1 cup diced tomatoes
- Juice and zest of 1 lemon
- 1/4 cup fresh dill, chopped
- 1/2 teaspoon dried thyme
- Salt and black pepper, to taste

Aegean Seafood Soup with Fennel and Lemon

 15 mins   30 min   4

O1   Heat olive oil in a large pot over medium heat. Sauté fennel, onion, and garlic for 5 minutes until softened.

O2   Add fish stock, tomatoes, thyme, lemon juice, and zest. Simmer for 15 minutes. Add mixed seafood and cook for 5-10 minutes until tender.

O3   Season with salt, pepper, and stir in dill. Serve hot, garnished with lemon zest or dill.

NUTRITIONAL VALUE	220 calories, 25g protein, 8g carbohydrates, 9g fat, 2g fiber, 120mg cholesterol, 450mg sodium, 700mg potassium.

Italian Monkfish Piccata

🕐 10 mins   🍲 20 min   👨 4

01 Season monkfish fillets with salt and pepper. Dredge in almond flour.

02 Heat olive oil in a skillet over medium-high. Cook monkfish for 3-4 minutes per side until golden. Remove and set aside.

03 Add lemon juice, chicken broth, and capers to the skillet. Simmer and scrape up browned bits. Stir in parsley and butter until sauce thickens. Return monkfish, spoon sauce over, and cook 2 more minutes. Serve hot.

INGREDIENTS

- 1.5 lbs monkfish fillets
- 1/4 cup almond flour
- 2 tbsp olive oil, salt and pepper
- 1/4 cup lemon juice
- 1/2 cup chicken broth
- 1/4 cup capers, drained
- 2 tbsp fresh parsley, chopped
- 2 tablespoons butter

NUTRITIONAL VALUE

310 calories, 32g protein, 4g carbohydrates, 18g fat, 2g fiber, 90mg cholesterol, 380mg sodium, 550mg potassium.

Cretan Shrimp with Feta and Tomatoes

🕐 10 mins   🍲 20 min   👦 4

01 Heat olive oil in a skillet over medium heat. Add onion and garlic, sauté until translucent.

02 Add diced tomatoes and oregano, cook for 5-7 minutes until sauce thickens. Add shrimp, cook for 4-5 minutes until pink.

03 Sprinkle feta over the shrimp mixture, cook for 2-3 minutes until cheese melts. Season with salt and pepper, garnish with parsley, and serve hot.

INGREDIENTS

- 1 pound large shrimp, peeled and deveined, 2 tablespoons olive oil
- 1 small onion, finely chopped
- 2 cloves garlic, minced, salt, pepper
- 1 can (14.5 ounces) diced tomatoes, drained, 1/2 cup crumbled feta cheese
- 1/4 cup fresh parsley, chopped
- 1 teaspoon dried oregano

NUTRITIONAL VALUE

250 calories, 25g protein, 6g carbohydrates, 14g fat, 2g fiber, 190mg cholesterol, 600mg sodium, 500mg potassium.

INGREDIENTS

- 4 tuna steaks (6 ounces each)
- 2 tbsp olive oil, salt and pepper
- I cup pitted Kalamata olives
- 1/4 cup fresh parsley, chopped
- 2 cloves garlic, minced
- 2 tablespoons capers, drained
- 2 tablespoons lemon juice
- 1/4 cup olive oil

Seared Tuna with Olive Tapenade

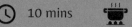 10 mins   10 min   4

01 For the tapenade, pulse Kalamata olives, parsley, garlic, capers, lemon juice, and 1/4 cup olive oil in a food processor until chunky. Season with salt and pepper. Set aside.

02 Heat 2 tablespoons olive oil in a skillet over medium-high. Season tuna with salt and pepper. Sear for 2-3 minutes per side.

03 Let tuna rest for a few minutes. Serve topped with tapenade and garnish with parsley if desired.

NUTRITIONAL VALUE | 350 calories, 35g protein, 3g carbohydrates, 22g fat, 2g fiber, 65mg cholesterol, 500mg sodium, 600mg potassium.

INGREDIENTS

- 2 pounds fresh mussels, cleaned and debearded, 2 tablespoons olive oil
- I small fennel bulb, thinly sliced
- 2 cloves garlic, minced
- 1/2 cup ouzo
- I cup cherry tomatoes, halved
- 1/2 cup chicken broth
- 1/4 cup fresh parsley, chopped
- Salt and pepper, to taste

28

Greek Mussels with Ouzo and Fennel

 10 mins   15 min   4

01 Heat olive oil in a large pot over medium heat. Add fennel and garlic, sauté until softened.

02 Pour in ouzo, cook for 1-2 minutes to evaporate the alcohol. Add cherry tomatoes and chicken broth, bring to a simmer.

03 Add mussels, cover, and cook for 5-7 minutes until they open. Discard any unopened mussels. Season with salt, pepper, and garnish with parsley before serving.

NUTRITIONAL VALUE | 180 calories, 18g protein, 7g carbohydrates, 7g fat, 2g fiber, 45mg cholesterol, 600mg sodium, 600mg potassium.

VEGETARIAN DISHES

INGREDIENTS

- 4 medium beetroots, washed and trimmed, 2 tbsp tahini, 2 tbsp olive oil
- 1 tablespoon lemon juice
- 1 garlic clove, minced
- 1 tsp cumin, 1/2 tsp coriander
- Salt and pepper, to taste
- Fresh parsley, chopped (for garnish)

Egyptian Spiced Beetroot Dip

 15 mins 45 min 4

O1 Preheat oven to 400°F (200°C). Wrap beetroots in foil and roast for 45 minutes until tender. Allow to cool, then peel and chop.

O2 In a food processor, blend roasted beetroots, tahini, olive oil, lemon juice, garlic, cumin, and coriander until smooth.

O3 Season with salt and pepper. Transfer to a serving bowl and garnish with chopped parsley and sesame seeds if desired.

NUTRITIONAL VALUE	150 calories, 2g protein, 11g carbohydrates, 11g fat, 3g fiber, 0mg cholesterol, 120mg sodium, 350mg potassium.

INGREDIENTS

- 1 medium head of cauliflower, chopped, 4 cups kale, chopped
- 1 small onion, diced
- 3 cloves garlic, minced
- 4 cups chicken or vegetable broth
- 1/4 cup olive oil
- 1 tsp thyme, 1/2 tsp rosemary
- 1/2 tsp chili flakes (optional)
- Salt and black pepper, to taste
- 1/4 cup grated Parmesan cheese

Tuscan Kale and Cauliflower Soup

 15 mins 30 min 4

O1 Heat olive oil in a pot over medium heat. Sauté onion and garlic for 5 minutes. Add cauliflower, thyme, rosemary, chili flakes, salt, and pepper. Sauté another 5 minutes.

O2 Pour in broth, bring to a boil, then simmer for 15 minutes until cauliflower is tender. Add kale and cook for 5 minutes until wilted.

O3 Optionally blend the soup to a smooth consistency. Serve hot, garnished with Parmesan cheese if desired.

NUTRITIONAL VALUE	180 calories, 5g protein, 12g carbohydrates, 13g fat, 5g fiber, 0mg cholesterol, 700mg sodium, 600mg potassium.

Mediterranean Stuffed Bell Peppers

🕐 15 mins   🍲 30 min   👤 4

01   Preheat oven to 375°F (190°C). Place bell pepper halves in a baking dish, cut side up.

02   Heat olive oil in a skillet over medium heat. Sauté onion and garlic for 5 minutes. Add ground beef or lamb, cooking until browned, about 8-10 minutes. Stir in diced tomatoes, olives, oregano, basil, salt, and pepper. Cook for 5 minutes until well combined.

03   Spoon the mixture into bell pepper halves and top with feta cheese. Bake for 25-30 minutes until peppers are tender and cheese is slightly golden. Garnish with fresh parsley before serving.

INGREDIENTS

- 4 large bell peppers, halved and seeds removed, 1 lb ground beef or lamb, 1 small onion, diced, 2 cloves garlic, minced, 1 cup diced tomatoes
- 1/4 cup Kalamata olives, sliced
- 1/4 cup crumbled feta cheese
- 2 tbsp olive oil, 1 tsp oregano, basil
- Salt and black pepper, to taste
- Fresh parsley, chopped, for garnish

NUTRITIONAL VALUE	320 calories, 20g protein, 12g carbohydrates, 22g fat, 4g fiber, 70mg cholesterol, 500mg sodium, 600mg potassium.

Eggplant Rollatini with Ricotta and Spinach

🕐 20 mins   🍲 30 min   👤 4

01   Preheat oven to 375°F (190°C). Line a baking sheet with parchment paper, arrange eggplant slices, brush with olive oil, season with salt and pepper, and roast for 10 minutes.

02   In a bowl, mix ricotta cheese, spinach, Parmesan, egg, basil, oregano, salt, and pepper.

03   Spread marinara sauce in a baking dish. Place ricotta mixture on each eggplant slice, roll up, and place seam side down in the dish. Top with remaining sauce and mozzarella cheese. Bake for 20 minutes until cheese is melted and bubbly. Let cool before serving.

INGREDIENTS

- 2 medium eggplants, 1 tbsp olive oil, 1 cup ricotta cheese, 1 cup fresh spinach, chopped, 1 large egg, 1/4 cup grated Parmesan
- 1 tsp dried basil, oregano
- Salt and black pepper, to taste
- 1 cup marinara sauce (no sugar)
- 1/2 cup shredded mozzarella cheese

NUTRITIONAL VALUE	240 calories, 12g protein, 10g carbohydrates, 18g fat, 4g fiber, 70mg cholesterol, 400mg sodium, 450mg potassium.

INGREDIENTS

- 1 medium cauliflower, chopped into florets, 1/2 cup almond flour
- 1/4 cup slivered almonds, toasted
- 1/4 cup grated Parmesan cheese
- 1/2 cup shredded mozzarella cheese
- 1/4 cup olive oil
- 3 cloves garlic, minced
- 1/4 cup fresh parsley, chopped
- 1 tsp dried oregano, salt and pepper
- 1/4 teaspoon red pepper flakes

Sicilian Cauliflower and Almond Casserole

🕐 15 mins   🍲 25 min   👤 4

O1 Preheat oven to 375°F (190°C) and grease a baking dish. Boil cauliflower florets in salted water for 5-7 minutes. Drain and transfer to the dish.

O2 Heat olive oil in a skillet over medium heat. Cook garlic for 1-2 minutes until fragrant. In a bowl, combine almond flour, toasted almonds, Parmesan, mozzarella, parsley, oregano, salt, black pepper, and red pepper flakes. Add garlic and olive oil, stirring to combine.

O3 Sprinkle the almond mixture over the cauliflower. Bake for 20-25 minutes until golden brown. Let cool slightly before serving.

NUTRITIONAL VALUE	280 calories, 10g protein, 8g carbohydrates, 24g fat, 4g fiber, 15mg cholesterol, 350mg sodium, 400mg potassium.

INGREDIENTS

- 2 medium zucchinis, thinly sliced
- 2 medium tomatoes, thinly sliced
- 1/2 cup grated Parmesan cheese
- 1/4 cup almond flour
- 2 cloves garlic, minced
- 1/4 cup fresh basil, chopped
- 1/4 cup olive oil, 1 tsp dried thyme
- Salt and black pepper, to taste

Provençal Zucchini and Tomato Gratin

🕐 15 mins   🍲 25 min   👤 4

O1 Preheat the oven to 375°F (190°C) and grease a baking dish with olive oil. Arrange alternating slices of zucchini and tomato in the dish, overlapping them slightly.

O2 In a small bowl, combine Parmesan, almond flour, garlic, basil, thyme, salt, and pepper. Sprinkle the mixture over the vegetables and drizzle with olive oil.

O3 Bake for 25 minutes until the vegetables are tender and the top is golden brown. Let cool slightly before serving.

NUTRITIONAL VALUE	200 calories, 7g protein, 8g carbohydrates, 16g fat, 3g fiber, 10mg cholesterol, 320mg sodium, 400mg potassium.

Spanish Chard and Manchego Omelette

 10 mins   15 min   4

01 Whisk eggs with salt and black pepper in a large bowl. Set aside.

02 Heat olive oil in a nonstick skillet over medium heat. Sauté onion and garlic for 5 minutes. Add Swiss chard and cook for 2-3 minutes until wilted.

03 Pour eggs into the skillet and stir gently. Cook for 2 minutes until eggs start to set. Sprinkle with Manchego cheese. Bake at 350°F for 8-10 minutes until set and golden. Serve warm.

INGREDIENTS

- 6 large eggs
- 1 cup Swiss chard, chopped
- 1/2 cup grated Manchego cheese
- 1 small onion, finely chopped
- 2 cloves garlic, minced
- 2 tablespoons olive oil
- Salt and black pepper, to taste

NUTRITIONAL VALUE

220 calories, 14g protein, 4g carbohydrates, 16g fat, 1g fiber, 280mg cholesterol, 320mg sodium, 400mg potassium.

Keto Falafel with Tzatziki Dipping Sauce

 20 mins   15 min   4

01 In a large bowl, combine cauliflower rice, almond flour, parsley, cilantro, garlic, onion, cumin, coriander, baking powder, salt, and pepper.

02 Add beaten eggs and mix well. Form into small patties. Heat olive oil in a skillet over medium heat. Fry patties until golden brown, 3-4 minutes per side. Drain on paper towels.

03 Combine Greek yogurt, grated cucumber, garlic, dill, lemon juice, salt, and pepper. Serve falafel warm with tzatziki sauce.

INGREDIENTS

- 2 cups cauliflower rice, 1/2 cup almond flour, salt and pepper
- 1/4 cup parsley, cilantro, chopped
- 2 cloves garlic, minced, 1 tsp baking powder, 1 onion, chopped
- 1 tbsp cumin, coriander, 2 large eggs, beaten, 2 tbsp olive oil
- 1 cup full-fat Greek yogurt, 1/2 cucumber, grated, 2 cloves garlic, minced 1 tbsp fresh dill, chopped
- 1 tbsp lemon juice

NUTRITIONAL VALUE

220 calories, 10g protein, 8g carbohydrates, 16g fat, 3g fiber, 60mg cholesterol, 320mg sodium, 300mg potassium.

INGREDIENTS

- 1 cup almond flour
- 2 cups vegetable broth
- 1/2 cup coconut cream
- 1/4 cup nutritional yeast
- 2 tbsp vegan butter, 1 tbsp olive oil
- 1 pound mushrooms, sliced
- 2 garlic cloves, minced
- 1 tablespoon fresh thyme, chopped
- Salt and pepper, to taste

Venetian Polenta with Roasted Mushrooms

🕐 10 mins   🍲 25 min   👤 4

01 Preheat oven to 400°F (200°C). Toss mushrooms with olive oil, garlic, thyme, salt, and pepper. Spread on a baking sheet and roast for 15-20 minutes until golden brown.

02 In a saucepan, bring vegetable broth to a boil. Reduce heat and whisk in almond flour until smooth.

03 Stir in coconut cream, nutritional yeast, and vegan butter. Cook, stirring frequently, until thickened, about 5-7 minutes. Serve the creamy polenta topped with roasted mushrooms.

NUTRITIONAL VALUE

290 calories, 6g protein, 9g carbohydrates, 24g fat, 4g fiber, 0mg cholesterol, 370mg sodium, 300mg potassium.

INGREDIENTS

- 4 large portobello mushrooms, stems removed
- 1/2 cup prepared basil pesto
- 1/4 cup grated Parmesan cheese
- 1/4 cup pine nuts, toasted
- 2 tablespoons olive oil
- Salt and black pepper, to taste

Italian Portobello Mushrooms with Pesto

🕐 10 mins   🍲 15 min   👤 4

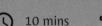

01 Preheat the oven to 375°F (190°C) and line a baking sheet with parchment paper. Brush portobello mushrooms with olive oil, season with salt and pepper, and place gill side up on the baking sheet.

02 Spread basil pesto on each mushroom, and sprinkle with Parmesan cheese and toasted pine nuts.

03 Bake for 12-15 minutes until mushrooms are tender and cheese is melted and golden. Serve warm.

NUTRITIONAL VALUE

280 calories, 8g protein, 7g carbohydrates, 24g fat, 3g fiber, 10mg cholesterol, 350mg sodium, 500mg potassium.

Lebanese Cauliflower Tabbouleh

🕐 15 mins   🍲 0 min   🧑 4

INGREDIENTS

- 1 medium head cauliflower, riced
- 1 cup fresh parsley, finely chopped
- 1/2 cup fresh mint, finely chopped
- 1/2 cup cherry tomatoes, diced
- 1 small cucumber, diced
- 1/4 cup red onion, finely chopped
- 1/4 cup olive oil, 1/4 cup lemon juice
- Salt and black pepper, to taste

O1   In a large bowl, combine riced cauliflower, chopped parsley, chopped mint, diced cherry tomatoes, diced cucumber, and chopped red onion.

O2   In a small bowl, whisk together olive oil, lemon juice, salt, and black pepper. Pour the dressing over the cauliflower mixture and toss well to combine.

O3   Let the tabbouleh sit for 10-15 minutes to allow the flavors to meld. Serve chilled or at room temperature.

NUTRITIONAL VALUE

120 calories, 3g protein, 8g carbohydrates, 9g fat, 4g fiber, 0mg cholesterol, 180mg sodium, 300mg potassium.

Moroccan Pumpkin and Goat Cheese Salad

 10 mins   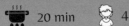 20 min   4

INGREDIENTS

- 2 cups pumpkin, peeled and cubed
- 2 tbsp olive oil, salt and pepper
- 1 tsp cumin, coriander, 1/2 tsp cinnamon, 4 cups mixed greens
- 1/4 cup crumbled goat cheese
- 1/4 cup roasted pumpkin seeds
- 1/4 cup pomegranate seeds
- 2 tbsp fresh cilantro, chopped
- 2 tablespoons lemon juice

O1   Preheat the oven to 400°F (200°C). Toss cubed pumpkin with olive oil, ground cumin, ground coriander, ground cinnamon, salt, and black pepper. Spread on a baking sheet and roast for 20 minutes until tender and slightly caramelized. Let cool.

O2   In a large salad bowl, combine mixed greens, crumbled goat cheese, roasted pumpkin seeds, pomegranate seeds (if using), and roasted pumpkin cubes.

O3   Drizzle with lemon juice and toss gently to combine. Garnish with fresh cilantro and serve immediately

NUTRITIONAL VALUE

220 calories, 6g protein, 12g carbohydrates, 16g fat, 4g fiber, 15mg cholesterol, 320mg sodium, 450mg potassium.

INGREDIENTS

- 2 large red bell peppers
- 1/2 cup almonds, toasted
- 2 cloves garlic, minced
- 1/4 cup olive oil
- 1 tablespoon red wine vinegar
- 1 teaspoon smoked paprika
- Salt and black pepper, to taste

Roasted Red Pepper and Almond Dip

 10 mins 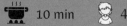 10 min   4

01 Preheat oven to 400°F (200°C). Roast red bell peppers on a baking sheet for 20 minutes, turning occasionally. Place in a bowl, cover with plastic wrap for 10 minutes, then peel and remove seeds.

02 In a food processor, combine roasted peppers, toasted almonds, garlic, olive oil, red wine vinegar, and smoked paprika. Process until smooth. Season with salt and black pepper.

03 Transfer dip to a bowl and serve with fresh vegetables or keto-friendly crackers.

NUTRITIONAL VALUE

180 calories, 4g protein, 7g carbohydrates, 15g fat, 3g fiber, 0mg cholesterol, 150mg sodium, 250mg potassium.

INGREDIENTS

- 2 medium eggplants, diced
- 1/4 cup olive oil, 1 onion, finely chopped, 2 cloves garlic, minced
- 2 celery stalks, chopped
- 1/2 cup canned diced tomatoes
- 2 tbsp capers, drained, salt, pepper
- 1/4 cup green olives, sliced
- 2 tbsp red wine vinegar
- 1 tbsp pine nuts, toasted
- Fresh basil leaves, for garnish

Aubergine Caponata with Pine Nuts

🕐 15 mins 🍲 30 min 👤 4

01 Heat olive oil in a skillet over medium heat. Cook diced aubergines (eggplants) until they begin to soften, about 10 minutes. Add chopped onion, minced garlic, and chopped celery. Cook until tender, about 5 minutes.

02 Stir in diced tomatoes, capers, olives, and red wine vinegar. Simmer for 15 minutes until thickened. Season with salt and pepper. Stir in toasted pine nuts.

03 Garnish with fresh basil leaves. Serve warm or at room temperature.

NUTRITIONAL VALUE

180 calories, 3g protein, 12g carbohydrates, 14g fat, 5g fiber, 0mg cholesterol, 300mg sodium, 450mg potassium.

Portuguese Kale and Almond Soup

 10 mins   25 min   4

INGREDIENTS

- 1 tablespoon olive oil
- 1 small onion, chopped
- 2 cloves garlic, minced
- 1/2 cup blanched almonds
- 6 cups chicken or vegetable broth
- 4 cups kale, chopped
- 1/2 teaspoon smoked paprika
- Salt and black pepper, to taste
- 1/4 cup fresh parsley, chopped

O1 Heat olive oil in a large pot over medium heat. Add chopped onion and minced garlic, cooking until softened, about 5 minutes.

O2 Add blanched almonds and cook for another 2-3 minutes, stirring frequently. Pour in chicken or vegetable broth and bring to a boil. Reduce heat and simmer for 10 minutes.

O3 Add chopped kale and smoked paprika, cooking until the kale is tender, about 10 minutes. Season with salt and black pepper to taste.

NUTRITIONAL VALUE

200 calories, 7g protein, 10g carbohydrates, 15g fat, 4g fiber, 0mg cholesterol, 450mg sodium, 500mg potassium.

Venetian Asparagus and Egg Salad

 15 mins   10 min   4

INGREDIENTS

- 1 pound asparagus, trimmed and cut into 2inch pieces
- 4 large eggs, 1/4 cup olive oil
- 2 tablespoons lemon juice
- 1 teaspoon Dijon mustard
- Salt and black pepper, to taste
- 1/4 cup grated Parmesan cheese
- 2 tbsp fresh parsley, chopped

O1 Bring a pot of salted water to a boil. Cook asparagus for 2-3 minutes until tender-crisp. Drain and rinse under cold water. In a separate pot, boil eggs for 8-10 minutes until hardboiled. Let cool, peel, and chop.

O2 In a small bowl, whisk together olive oil, lemon juice, Dijon mustard, salt, and pepper for the dressing. In a large bowl, combine asparagus, chopped eggs, and grated Parmesan. Drizzle with dressing and toss to combine.

O3 Garnish with fresh parsley and serve immediately.

NUTRITIONAL VALUE

220 calories, 10g protein, 7g carbohydrates, 18g fat, 3g fiber, 210mg cholesterol, 250mg sodium, 400mg potassium.

INGREDIENTS

- 4 medium zucchinis
- 1/2 pound ground beef or lamb
- 1/2 cup walnuts, finely chopped
- I small onion, finely chopped
- 2 cloves garlic, minced
- I tbsp olive oil, I tsp cumin, coriander
- 1/2 tsp cinnamon, salt and pepper
- 1/4 cup fresh parsley, chopped
- 1/4 cup tomato sauce (no sugar)

Stuffed Zucchini with Walnuts and Spices

 20 mins 30 min 4

O1 Preheat oven to 375°F (190°C). Halve zucchinis lengthwise and scoop out flesh to create boats. Set aside.

O2 Heat olive oil in a skillet over medium heat. Cook onion and garlic for 5 minutes. Add ground beef or lamb and cook until browned, 8-10 minutes. Stir in walnuts, cumin, coriander, cinnamon, salt, and pepper. Cook for 2 more minutes, then stir in parsley.

O3 Fill zucchinis with meat mixture and place in a baking dish. Top with tomato sauce. Cover with foil and bake for 25-30 minutes until tender. Serve warm.

NUTRITIONAL VALUE	280 calories, 16g protein, 8g carbohydrates, 20g fat, 3g fiber, 45mg cholesterol, 350mg sodium, 500mg potassium.

INGREDIENTS

- I cup almond flour, 1/4 cup coconut flour, 1/4 cup butter, melted
- 4 large eggs, I cup crumbled feta cheese, 2 cups spinach, chopped
- 1/4 cup grated Parmesan cheese
- 1/4 cup heavy cream
- I small onion, finely chopped
- 2 cloves garlic, minced
- I tsp dried dill, salt and pepper

Macedonian Spinach and Feta Pie

 15 mins 30 min 4

O1 Preheat oven to 350°F (175°C) and grease a pie dish with butter. Mix almond flour, coconut flour, and melted butter until dough-like. Press into the dish to form a crust.

O2 Heat oil in a skillet over medium heat. Cook onion and garlic for 5 minutes, then add spinach and cook until wilted, 2-3 minutes. Whisk eggs, feta, Parmesan, heavy cream, dill, salt, and pepper in a bowl. Stir in the spinach mixture.

O3 Pour over the crust and bake for 25-30 minutes until golden brown and set. Let cool slightly before serving.

NUTRITIONAL VALUE	320 calories, 14g protein, 8g carbohydrates, 26g fat, 4g fiber, 180mg cholesterol, 450mg sodium, 350mg potassium.

MEATS & POULTRY

INGREDIENTS

- 1 lb ground lamb, 1 onion, chopped
- 2 cloves garlic, minced
- 1/4 cup fresh parsley, chopped
- 1 tsp ground cumin, coriander
- 1/2 tsp ground cinnamon
- Salt and black pepper, to taste
- 2 tbsp olive oil, 1 cup full-fat Greek yogurt, 1/2 cucumber, grated
- 2 cloves garlic, minced, 1 tbsp dill, 1 tbsp lemon juice, salt and pepper

Greek Lamb Koftas with Tzatziki Sauce

 15 mins 15 min 4

O1 Combine ground lamb, onion, garlic, parsley, cumin, coriander, cinnamon, salt, and pepper in a bowl. Form into small patties or meatballs.

O2 Heat olive oil in a skillet over medium heat. Cook koftas for 7-8 minutes on each side until browned and cooked through.

O3 Prepare tzatziki by mixing Greek yogurt, grated cucumber, garlic, dill, lemon juice, salt, and pepper. Serve lamb koftas hot with tzatziki.

NUTRITIONAL VALUE
350 calories, 22g protein, 6g carbohydrates, 27g fat, 1g fiber, 80mg cholesterol, 450mg sodium, 400mg potassium.

INGREDIENTS

- 4 large bell peppers, halved and seeds removed, 1 tbsp olive oil
- 1/2 pound chorizo sausage, diced
- 1 small onion, finely chopped
- 2 cloves garlic, minced
- 1 cup grated Manchego cheese
- 1/2 cup diced tomatoes
- 1 tsp smoked paprika, salt and pepper

Chorizo and Manchego Stuffed Peppers

 15 mins 30 min 4

O1 Preheat oven to 375°F (190°C). Place bell pepper halves in a baking dish, cut side up.

O2 Heat olive oil in a skillet over medium heat. Cook chorizo, onion, and garlic for 5-7 minutes until softened and browned. Stir in tomatoes and paprika, cooking for 2-3 more minutes.

O3 Spoon mixture into bell peppers, top with Manchego cheese, and bake for 25-30 minutes until tender and golden. Serve hot.

NUTRITIONAL VALUE
320 calories, 18g protein, 8g carbohydrates, 24g fat, 2g fiber, 60mg cholesterol, 600mg sodium, 400mg potassium.

Chicken Cacciatore with Olives and Capers

🕐 15 mins　　🍲 40 min　　👤 4

O1 Heat olive oil in a large skillet over medium-high heat. Season chicken thighs with salt and pepper. Brown on all sides, about 5 minutes per side. Remove and set aside.

O2 In the same skillet, sauté onion, garlic, and bell pepper until softened, about 5 minutes. Add diced tomatoes, chicken broth, olives, capers, oregano, and basil. Stir to combine, then return chicken to the skillet.

O3 Reduce heat to low, cover, and simmer for 30 minutes until chicken is cooked through and tender. Garnish with fresh parsley before serving.

INGREDIENTS

- 1 1/2 lb chicken thighs, skinless and bone-in, 2 tbsp olive oil
- 1 small onion, finely chopped, 2 cloves garlic, minced, 1 bell pepper, chopped, 1 cup canned diced tomatoes, 2 tbsp capers, drained
- 1/2 cup chicken broth, 1/4 cup Kalamata olives, pitted and sliced
- 1 tsp dried oregano, basil
- Salt and black pepper, to taste
- Fresh parsley, chopped, for garnish

NUTRITIONAL VALUE	350 calories, 28g protein, 8g carbohydrates, 22g fat, 2g fiber, 110mg cholesterol, 700mg sodium, 450mg potassium.

Turkish Beef Kebabs with Sumac Onions

🕐 20 mins　　🍲 15 min　　👤 4

O1 In a large bowl, combine ground beef, grated onion, minced garlic, parsley, cumin, paprika, coriander, salt, and black pepper. Mix well and shape into kebabs.

O2 Heat olive oil in a skillet over medium-high heat. Cook kebabs for 10-12 minutes, turning occasionally, until browned and cooked through.

O3 In a separate bowl, combine thinly sliced red onion, sumac, and lemon juice. Toss to coat the onions. Serve the beef kebabs hot, topped with sumac onions and extra parsley if desired.

INGREDIENTS

- 1 1/2 pounds ground beef
- 1 onion, grated, 2 cloves garlic, minced, salt and pepper
- 1/4 cup fresh parsley, chopped
- 1 tsp ground cumin, paprika
- 1/2 tsp coriander, 2 tbsp olive oil
- 1 large red onion, thinly sliced
- 1 tbsp sumac, 1 tbsp fresh lemon juice

NUTRITIONAL VALUE	320 calories, 24g protein, 8g carbohydrates, 22g fat, 2g fiber, 80mg cholesterol, 450mg sodium, 400mg potassium.

INGREDIENTS

- 1 1/2 pounds chicken thighs, skinless and bone-in, 2 tbsp olive oil
- 1 large onion, finely chopped
- 3 cloves garlic, minced
- 1 tsp cumin, ginger, turmeric
- 1/2 tsp cinnamon, 1 cup chicken broth
- 1 preserved lemon, sliced, 1/2 cup green olives, pitted
- 1/4 cup fresh cilantro, chopped
- Salt and black pepper, to taste

Moroccan Lemon and Olive Chicken Tagine

🕐 15 mins   🍲 45 min   👤 4

O1   Heat olive oil in a large tagine or heavy-bottomed pot over medium heat. Sauté chopped onion and minced garlic until softened, about 5 minutes.

O2   Add chicken thighs, browning on all sides for about 5-7 min. Stir in ground cumin, ginger, turmeric, and cinnamon. Cook for an additional 2 min until fragrant.

O3   Pour in chicken broth and bring to a simmer. Add preserved lemon slices and green olives. Cover and cook for 30-35 minutes until chicken is tender. Garnish with fresh cilantro before serving.

NUTRITIONAL VALUE   350 calories, 28g protein, 6g carbohydrates, 24g fat, 2g fiber, 110mg cholesterol, 800mg sodium, 450mg potassium.

INGREDIENTS

- 1 1/2 pounds chicken thighs, skinless and bone-in, 1/4 cup olive oil
- 3 cloves garlic, minced
- 1 tablespoon Piri-Piri sauce (or more, to taste), 1 tsp smoked paprika
- 1 teaspoon dried oregano
- Juice of 1 lemon
- Salt and black pepper, to taste
- Fresh parsley, chopped, for garnish

Portuguese Piri-Piri Grilled Chicken

🕐 10 mins   🍲 25 min   👤 4

O1   In a large bowl, combine olive oil, minced garlic, Piri-piri sauce, smoked paprika, dried oregano, lemon juice, salt, and black pepper. Add chicken thighs and toss to coat. Marinate for at least 1 hour or overnight.

O2   Preheat grill to medium-high heat. Grill chicken thighs for 6-8 minutes per side until they reach an internal temperature of 165°F (75°C) and are cooked through.

O3   Remove from the grill and let rest for a few minutes. Garnish with fresh chopped parsley and serve hot.

NUTRITIONAL VALUE   320 calories, 24g protein, 2g carbohydrates, 24g fat, 1g fiber, 90mg cholesterol, 400mg sodium, 350mg potassium.

Sicilian Pork Roulade with Pine Nuts and Raisins

 20 mins | 40 min | 4

O1 Preheat oven to 375°F (190°C). Combine pine nuts, raisins, Parmesan, garlic, and parsley in a bowl. Season with salt and pepper. Lay pork loin flat, spread mixture, roll tightly, and secure with twine.

O2 Heat olive oil in an ovenproof skillet over medium-high heat. Sear pork on all sides for 2-3 minutes per side. Add chicken broth and transfer to oven. Roast for 25-30 minutes until internal temperature reaches 145°F (63°C).

O3 Let the roulade rest for 10 minutes before slicing and serving.

NUTRITIONAL VALUE

360 calories, 28g protein, 8g carbohydrates, 24g fat, 2g fiber, 90mg cholesterol, 400mg sodium, 450mg potassium.

INGREDIENTS

- 1 1/2 pounds pork loin, butterflied
- 1/4 cup pine nuts, toasted
- 1/4 cup raisins, soaked in warm water and drained, 1/2 cup grated Parmesan, 2 cloves garlic, minced
- 1/4 cup fresh parsley, chopped
- 2 tablespoons olive oil
- Salt and black pepper, to taste
- 1/2 cup chicken broth

French Duck Confit with Thyme and Garlic

 15 mins | 2 hours | 4

O1 Rub duck legs with sea salt, crushed black peppercorns, garlic, and thyme. Place in a dish, cover, and refrigerate for 24 hours.

O2 Preheat oven to 225°F (110°C). Rinse duck legs to remove excess salt and pat dry. Melt duck fat in an ovenproof pot over low heat and submerge the duck legs.

O3 Cook in the oven for 2 hours or until the meat is tender and easily pulled from the bone. Remove from the oven, let cool slightly, and serve.

NUTRITIONAL VALUE

450 calories, 28g protein, 1g carbohydrates, 36g fat, 0g fiber, 130mg cholesterol, 600mg sodium, 400mg potassium.

INGREDIENTS

- 4 duck legs
- 2 tablespoons sea salt
- 1 tablespoon black peppercorns, crushed
- 8 cloves garlic, peeled and smashed
- 6 sprigs fresh thyme
- 4 cups duck fat (or enough to submerge the duck legs)

INGREDIENTS

- 1 1/2 pounds beef stew meat, cut into cubes, 1 large onion, finely chopped
- 2 tbsp olive oil, 3 cloves garlic, minced
- 2 tablespoons smoked paprika
- 1 tsp ground cumin, 1 tsp dried thyme
- 1 tsp rosemary, 4 cups beef broth
- 2 cups chopped tomatoes
- 2 bell peppers, chopped
- Salt and black pepper, to taste
- Fresh parsley, chopped, for garnish

Croatian Beef Stew with Smoked Paprika

 15 mins   90 min   4

O1 Heat olive oil in a pot over medium-high heat. Brown beef cubes for 5-7 minutes. Remove and set aside.

O2 Sauté onion and garlic in the same pot for 5 minutes. Stir in smoked paprika, cumin, thyme, and rosemary. Cook for 2 minutes.

O3 Return beef to the pot. Add beef broth, tomatoes, and bell peppers. Bring to a boil, reduce heat, cover, and simmer for 1 hour 30 minutes. Season with salt and pepper. Garnish with parsley before serving.

NUTRITIONAL VALUE	350 calories, 30g protein, 10g carbohydrates, 20g fat, 3g fiber, 90mg cholesterol, 600mg sodium, 700mg potassium.

INGREDIENTS

- 8 lamb chops, 2 tablespoons olive oil
- 1 tsp ground cumin, coriander
- 1 teaspoon ground cinnamon
- 1/2 teaspoon ground allspice
- 1 cup fullfat Greek yogurt
- 1/4 cup fresh mint, chopped
- 1 tablespoon lemon juice
- 1 clove garlic, minced
- Salt and black pepper, to taste

Egyptian Spiced Lamb Chops with Mint Yogurt

 15 mins   15 min   4

O1 In a small bowl, mix olive oil, cumin, coriander, cinnamon, allspice, salt, and pepper. Rub onto lamb chops and marinate for 15 minutes.

O2 Preheat a grill or skillet over medium-high heat. Cook lamb chops for 3-4 minutes per side for medium rare, or until desired doneness

O3 Prepare mint yogurt by combining Greek yogurt, chopped mint, lemon juice, minced garlic, salt, and pepper in a bowl. Serve lamb chops hot with a dollop of mint yogurt.

NUTRITIONAL VALUE	450 calories, 28g protein, 6g carbohydrates, 36g fat, 1g fiber, 110mg cholesterol, 450mg sodium, 400mg potassium.

Lebanese Chicken Shawarma Salad

🕐 20 mins   🍲 20 min   👤 4

01 In a large bowl, combine olive oil, minced garlic, cumin, paprika, turmeric, cinnamon, cayenne (if using), salt, and pepper. Add thinly sliced chicken breast and toss to coat. Marinate for 15 minutes.

02 Heat a large skillet over medium-high heat. Cook the marinated chicken for 5-7 minutes per side until fully cooked and slightly charred. Remove from heat, let rest, then slice into strips.

03 In a large salad bowl, combine mixed greens, cherry tomatoes, cucumber, red onion, Kalamata olives, and fresh parsley. Top with chicken strips.

NUTRITIONAL VALUE	350 calories, 30g protein, 10g carbohydrates, 20g fat, 3g fiber, 70mg cholesterol, 600mg sodium, 500mg potassium.

INGREDIENTS

- 1 1/2 pounds chicken breast, sliced
- 2 tbsp olive oil, 2 cloves garlic, minced, 1 tsp ground cumin, paprika, 1/2 tsp ground turmeric, cinnamon, 1/4 tsp cayenne pepper, salt, pepper, 4 cups mixed greens
- 1/2 cup cherry tomatoes, halved
- 1/2 cucumber, sliced 1/4 red onion, thinly sliced 1/4 cup Kalamata olives, pitted and sliced 1/4 cup fresh parsley, chopped 1/4 cup tahini dressing

Israeli Chicken Schnitzel with Za'atar

🕐 20 mins   🍲 15 min   👤 4

01 Place chicken breasts between plastic wrap and pound to an even thickness. Mix almond flour, za'atar, garlic powder, onion powder, salt, and pepper. Beat eggs in a separate bowl.

02 Dip chicken in egg, then coat with almond flour mixture. Heat olive oil in a skillet over medium heat. Fry chicken for 4-5 minutes per side until golden and cooked through.

03 Serve with lemon wedges and parsley.

NUTRITIONAL VALUE	300 calories, 35g protein, 5g carbohydrates, 15g fat, 2g fiber, 125mg cholesterol, 350mg sodium, 400mg potassium.

INGREDIENTS

- 4 boneless, skinless chicken breasts
- 1 cup almond flour
- 2 tablespoons za'atar seasoning
- 1 teaspoon garlic powder
- 1 teaspoon onion powder
- Salt and pepper, to taste
- 2 large eggs, 1/4 cup olive oil
- Lemon wedges, chopped parsley

INGREDIENTS

- 2 medium eggplants, sliced into 1/4inch rounds, 2 tbsp olive oil
- I lb ground lamb, I onion, chopped
- 3 cloves garlic, minced
- I tsp ground cinnamon, cumin
- I cup diced tomatoes (canned)
- 1/4 cup fresh parsley, chopped
- Salt and black pepper, to taste
- I cup ricotta cheese, I large egg
- 1/2 cup grated Parmesan cheese

Moussaka with Eggplant and Ground Lamb

 20 mins   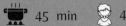 45 min   4

O1 Preheat oven to 375°F (190°C). Brush eggplant slices with olive oil, season, and bake for 15 minutes until tender.

O2 Cook ground lamb in a skillet until browned. Add onion, garlic, cinnamon, and cumin; cook for 5 minutes. Stir in tomatoes and parsley, season, and simmer for 10 minutes.

O3 Combine ricotta, Parmesan, and egg in a bowl. Layer half the eggplant, lamb mixture, and remaining eggplant in a baking dish. Top with ricotta mixture. Bake for 25-30 minutes until golden. Serve cooled.

NUTRITIONAL VALUE	350 calories, 25g protein, 10g carbohydrates, 24g fat, 4g fiber, 90mg cholesterol, 500mg sodium, 600mg potassium.

INGREDIENTS

- I 1/2 pounds lamb shoulder, cut into chunks, 2 tablespoons olive oil
- I large onion, finely chopped
- 3 cloves garlic, minced
- 2 cups full-fat Greek yogurt
- 2 large eggs, I tsp dried oregano
- Salt and black pepper, to taste
- Fresh parsley, chopped, for garnish

Albanian Baked Lamb and Yogurt

 15 min   90 min   4

O1 Preheat oven to 350°F (175°C). Heat olive oil in an ovenproof skillet over medium-high heat. Brown lamb chunks for 5-7 minutes. Remove and set aside.

O2 Sauté onion and garlic in the same skillet for 5 minutes. Return lamb, season with salt, pepper, and oregano.

O3 Whisk Greek yogurt and eggs in a bowl. Pour over lamb and stir. Bake for 1 hour and 30 minutes until lamb is tender and sauce is thickened. Garnish with parsley before serving.

NUTRITIONAL VALUE	420 calories, 28g protein, 6g carbohydrates, 32g fat, 1g fiber, 150mg cholesterol, 350mg sodium, 500mg potassium.

Turkish Meatballs in Tomato and Pepper Sauce

🕐 20 mins   🍲 40 min   🧑 4

01 Combine ground beef or lamb, onion, garlic, parsley, cumin, coriander, cinnamon, paprika, salt, and pepper. Form into meatballs.

02 Heat olive oil in a skillet over medium-high heat. Cook meatballs until browned, 5-7 minutes. Remove and set aside. Cook bell peppers in the same skillet for 5 minutes. Add tomatoes, tomato sauce, and oregano. Stir.

03 Return meatballs to the skillet, reduce heat to low, and simmer for 20-25 minutes until cooked through and sauce thickens. Serve hot, garnished with parsley.

NUTRITIONAL VALUE

350 calories, 25g protein, 10g carbohydrates, 24g fat, 3g fiber, 80mg cholesterol, 600mg sodium, 450mg potassium.

INGREDIENTS

- 1 lb ground beef or lamb, 1 onion, finely chopped, 2 cl. garlic, minced
- 1/4 cup fresh parsley, chopped
- 1 tsp cumin, coriander, oregano
- 1/2 tsp cinnamon, ground paprika
- Salt and black pepper, to taste
- 2 tbsp olive oil, 2 bell peppers, chopped 1 can (14.5 oz) diced tomatoes (no sugar added)
- 1/2 cup tomato sauce (no sugar)

Rabbit with Almonds and Sherry Vinegar

🕐 20 mins   🍲 60 min   🧑 4

01 Heat olive oil in a skillet over medium-high heat. Season rabbit with salt and pepper. Brown on all sides for 5-7 minutes. Remove and set aside.

02 Sauté onion and garlic in the same skillet for 5 minutes. Add almonds and cook for 2-3 minutes until toasted.

03 Add dry sherry, sherry vinegar, chicken broth, smoked paprika, and thyme, scraping up browned bits. Return rabbit to the skillet, reduce heat to low, cover, and simmer for 45 minutes to 1 hour until tender. Garnish with parsley before serving.

INGREDIENTS

- 1 whole rabbit, cut into pieces
- 1/4 cup olive oil, 1 onion, finely chopped, 3 cloves garlic, minced
- 1/2 cup blanched almonds, chopped, 1/2 cup dry sherry, 1/4 cup sherry vinegar, 1 cup chicken broth, 1 teaspoon smoked paprika
- 1 teaspoon dried thyme
- Salt and black pepper, to taste
- Fresh parsley, chopped, for garnish

NUTRITIONAL VALUE

380 calories, 30g protein, 6g carbohydrates, 24g fat, 2g fiber, 110mg cholesterol, 600mg sodium, 500mg potassium.

INGREDIENTS

- 1 1/2 pounds pork shoulder, cut into 1inch cubes
- 1/4 cup olive oil
- Juice of 1 lemon
- 3 cloves garlic, minced
- 1 tablespoon dried oregano
- 1 tablespoon dried thyme
- Salt and black pepper, to taste
- Fresh parsley, chopped, for garnish
- Lemon wedges, for serving

Cyprioi Pork Souvlaki with Lemon and Herbs

🕐 15 mins   🍲 15 min   👤 4

01 Combine olive oil, lemon juice, garlic, oregano, thyme, salt, and pepper in a bowl. Add pork cubes and marinate for 30 minutes.

02 Preheat grill to medium-high. Thread pork onto skewers and grill for 10-15 minutes, turning occasionally until cooked through and slightly charred.

03 Remove from grill, rest briefly, and garnish with parsley. Serve with lemon wedges and enjoy hot with a keto-friendly side dish.

NUTRITIONAL VALUE	350 calories, 28g protein, 3g carbohydrates, 24g fat, 1g fiber, 90mg cholesterol, 400mg sodium, 500mg potassium.

INGREDIENTS

- 1 whole rabbit, cut into pieces
- 1/4 cup olive oil, 1 large onion, finely chopped, 3 cloves garlic, minced
- 1 cup red wine, 1 cup chicken broth
- 1 can (14.5 oz) diced tomatoes
- 1/4 cup tomato paste, 1 tsp dried thyme, rosemary, 1 bay leaf
- Fresh parsley, chopped, for garnish
- 1 cup full-fat ricotta cheese
- 1/4 cup grated Parmesan cheese
- 1 large egg, 1 tbsp fresh mint, chopped
- Salt and black pepper, to taste

Maliese Rabbii Siew wiih Keio Gbejniei (Cheese)

🕐 20 min   🍲 90 min   👤 4

01 Heat olive oil in a pot over medium-high. Season and brown rabbit for 5-7 minutes, then set aside. Sauté onion and garlic for 5 minutes. Add wine, broth, tomatoes, paste, thyme, rosemary, and bay leaf. Return rabbit, bring to a boil, reduce heat, cover, and simmer for 1.5 hours.

02 Preheat oven to 375°F (190°C). Mix ricotta, Parmesan, egg, mint (if using), salt, and pepper. Spoon into greased ramekins. Bake for 20-25 minutes until golden.

03 Serve rabbit stew hot, garnished with parsley, alongside the keto gbejniet.

NUTRITIONAL VALUE	420 calories, 32g protein, 8g carbohydrates, 26g fat, 3g fiber, 140mg cholesterol, 700mg sodium, 500mg potassium.

SOUPS

INGREDIENTS

- 1 tablespoon olive oil
- 1/2 pound chorizo sausage, sliced
- 1 small onion, finely chopped
- 2 cloves garlic, minced
- 1 tsp smoked paprika, 4 cups chicken broth, 2 cups chopped kale
- 1 cup diced tomatoes (canned, no sugar added), salt and black pepper

Tuscan Kale and Chorizo Soup

 15 mins   30 min   4

01 Heat olive oil in a pot over medium heat. Cook sliced chorizo until browned, about 5 minutes. Remove and set aside.

02 In the same pot, sauté onion and garlic for 5 minutes until softened. Stir in smoked paprika.

03 Add chicken broth, kale, diced tomatoes, and browned chorizo. Bring to a boil, then reduce heat and simmer for 20 minutes. Season with salt and pepper to taste. Serve hot.

NUTRITIONAL VALUE 280 calories, 15g protein, 8g carbohydrates, 20g fat, 3g fiber, 40mg cholesterol, 800mg sodium, 600mg potassium.

INGREDIENTS

- 6 cups chicken broth, 1 pound boneless, skinless chicken thighs, 3 large eggs, 1/4 cup fresh lemon juice
- 1/2 cup cauliflower rice
- 1 cup spinach, chopped
- 1 small onion, finely chopped
- 2 cloves garlic, minced
- Salt and black pepper, to taste
- Fresh dill, chopped, for garnish

Greek Lemon Chicken Soup (Avgolemono)

 15 mins   25 min   4

01 In a large pot, bring chicken broth to a boil. Add chicken thighs, simmer for 15-20 minutes until cooked. Remove, shred, and set aside. Whisk eggs and lemon juice in a bowl, gradually add hot broth to temper.

02 Stir cauliflower rice, spinach, onion, and garlic into the pot. Cook for 5 minutes until tender. Reduce heat to low and slowly stir in the egg mixture. Return shredded chicken to the pot and season with salt and pepper.

03 Serve hot, garnished with fresh dill.

NUTRITIONAL VALUE 250 calories, 28g protein, 6g carbohydrates, 12g fat, 2g fiber, 160mg cholesterol, 800mg sodium, 500mg potassium.

Roasted Red Pepper and Feta Soup

 15 mins   30 min   4

INGREDIENTS

- 4 large red bell peppers
- 2 tbsp olive oil, 1 onion, finely chopped, 3 cloves garlic, minced
- 4 cups chicken or vegetable broth
- 1/2 cup crumbled feta cheese
- 1 teaspoon smoked paprika
- 1/2 teaspoon dried oregano
- Salt and black pepper, to taste
- Fresh basil, chopped, for garnish

01 Preheat oven to 400°F (200°C). Roast bell peppers for 20-25 minutes until charred. Cover, cool, peel, seed, and chop.

02 Heat olive oil in a pot. Cook onion and garlic for 5 minutes. Add peppers, broth, paprika, and oregano. Boil, then simmer for 10 minutes

03 Puree soup until smooth. Stir in feta until melted. Season with salt and pepper. Serve hot, garnished with basil.

NUTRITIONAL VALUE

200 calories, 6g protein, 10g carbohydrates, 15g fat, 3g fiber, 25mg cholesterol, 800mg sodium, 500mg potassium.

Sicilian Seafood Stew with Herbs

 15 mins   30 min   4

INGREDIENTS

- 2 tbsp olive oil, 1 onion, chopped
- 2 cloves garlic, minced
- 1 can (14.5 oz) diced tomatoes
- 4 cups fish or seafood broth
- 1/2 cup dry white wine
- 1 tsp oregano, thyme, salt & pepper
- 1/2 tsp crushed red pepper flakes
- 1 lb white fish fillets, cut into chunks
- 1/2 lb shrimp, peeled and deveined
- 1/2 pound mussels, cleaned
- 1/2 pound squid, cut into rings
- Fresh parsley and basil, for garnish

01 Heat olive oil in a large pot over medium heat. Cook chopped onion and minced garlic for about 5 minutes until softened.

02 Add diced tomatoes, seafood broth, white wine, oregano, thyme, and red pepper flakes. Bring to a boil, then reduce heat and simmer for 10 minutes. Add fish fillets, shrimp, mussels, and squid. Cook for 10-12 minutes until seafood is cooked and mussels have opened.

03 Season with salt and pepper. Serve hot, garnished with fresh parsley and basil.

NUTRITIONAL VALUE

280 calories, 35g protein, 8g carbohydrates, 10g fat, 2g fiber, 150mg cholesterol, 800mg sodium, 600mg potassium.

INGREDIENTS

- 1 cup blanched almonds
- 2 cloves garlic, 2 cups cold water
- 1/4 cup extra virgin olive oil
- 2 tablespoons sherry vinegar
- 1 cucumber, peeled and chopped
- Salt to taste, 1/4 cup green grapes (optional garnish)
- Fresh chives, chopped (optional garnish)

Andalusian Chilled Almond Soup (Ajo Blanco)

🕐 15 mins   🍲 0 min   👤 4

O1 In a blender, combine blanched almonds, garlic, cold water, olive oil, sherry vinegar, and cucumber. Blend until smooth.

O2 Season with salt to taste. If too thick, add more cold water to achieve desired consistency. Chill in the refrigerator for at least 1 hour.

O3 Serve cold, garnished with green grapes and chopped chives if desired.

NUTRITIONAL VALUE	220 calories, 5g protein, 6g carbohydrates, 20g fat, 3g fiber, 0mg cholesterol, 150mg sodium, 250mg potassium.

INGREDIENTS

- 1 pound cod fillets, cut into chunks
- 2 tablespoons olive oil
- 1 small onion, finely chopped
- 2 cloves garlic, minced
- 1/2 teaspoon saffron threads
- 4 cups fish or chicken broth
- 1 cup heavy cream
- Salt and black pepper, to taste
- Fresh parsley, chopped, for garnish

Venetian Creamy Cod and Saffron Soup

🕐 15 mins   🍲 30 min   👤 4

O1 Heat olive oil in a large pot over medium heat. Cook chopped onion and minced garlic for about 5 minutes until softened.

O2 Stir in saffron threads and cook for another minute. Add fish or chicken broth, bring to a boil, then reduce heat and simmer for 10 minutes. Add cod chunks and cook until opaque and flaky, about 10 minutes.

O3 Stir in heavy cream, season with salt and black pepper, and simmer for another 5 minutes. Serve hot, garnished with fresh parsley.

NUTRITIONAL VALUE	320 calories, 25g protein, 8g carbohydrates, 22g fat, 1g fiber, 90mg cholesterol, 600mg sodium, 400mg potassium.

Provençal Tomato and Basil Soup

🕐 10 mins   🍲 30 min   👤 4

INGREDIENTS

- 2 tablespoons olive oil
- I small onion, finely chopped
- 3 cloves garlic, minced
- 6 large ripe tomatoes, chopped
- 4 cups chicken or vegetable broth
- 1/4 cup fresh basil leaves, chopped
- I tsp dried oregano, salt and pepper, 1/2 cup heavy cream
- Fresh basil leaves, for garnish

O1   Heat olive oil in a large pot over medium heat. Cook chopped onion and minced garlic for about 5 minutes until softened.

O2   Add chopped tomatoes, chicken or vegetable broth, fresh basil, and dried oregano. Bring to a boil, then reduce heat and simmer for 20 minutes.

O3   Use an immersion blender to puree the soup until smooth. Stir in heavy cream, if using, and season with salt and black pepper. Simmer for an additional 5 minutes. Serve hot, garnished with fresh basil leaves.

NUTRITIONAL VALUE

180 calories, 4g protein, 12g carbohydrates, 14g fat, 3g fiber, 20mg cholesterol, 800mg sodium, 500mg potassium.

Catalan Beef and Mushroom Broth

🕐 15 mins   🍲 45 min   👤 4

INGREDIENTS

- 2 tablespoons olive oil
- I pound beef stew meat, cut into small cubes, I onion, finely chopped, 2 cloves garlic, minced
- I cup mushrooms, sliced
- 6 cups beef broth
- I teaspoon dried thyme
- I teaspoon smoked paprika
- Salt and black pepper, to taste
- Fresh parsley, chopped, for garnish

O1   Heat olive oil in a pot over medium-high. Brown beef for 5-7 minutes, then set aside.

O2   Sauté onion and garlic for 5 minutes in the same pot. Add mushrooms, cook until browned, about 5 minutes. Return beef to pot, add broth, thyme, and paprika. Boil, reduce heat, and simmer for 30 minutes.

O3   Season with salt and pepper. Serve hot, garnished with parsley.

NUTRITIONAL VALUE

250 calories, 25g protein, 6g carbohydrates, 14g fat, 2g fiber, 60mg cholesterol, 800mg sodium, 400mg potassium.

INGREDIENTS

- 2 tablespoons olive oil
- I small onion, finely chopped
- 2 cloves garlic, minced
- 4 cups fresh spinach, chopped
- 4 cups chicken or vegetable broth
- I cup full-fat Greek yogurt
- I egg yolk, I tablespoon lemon juice
- Salt and black pepper, to taste
- Fresh dill, chopped, for garnish

Turkish Spinach and Yogurt Soup

 10 mins 20 min 4

O1 Heat olive oil in a pot over medium heat. Cook onion and garlic for 5 minutes. Add spinach and cook for 3 minutes. Pour in broth, bring to a boil, reduce heat, and simmer for 10 minutes.

O2 Whisk Greek yogurt, egg yolk, and lemon juice in a bowl. Slowly add hot broth to temper. Stir tempered mixture back into the pot. Cook on low for 5 minutes without boiling. Season with salt and pepper.

O3 Serve hot, garnished with fresh dill.

NUTRITIONAL VALUE

180 calories, 8g protein, 6g carbohydrates, 14g fat, 2g fiber, 60mg cholesterol, 600mg sodium, 400mg potassium.

INGREDIENTS

- 2 tbsp olive oil, I onion, chopped
- 2 cloves garlic, minced
- I tsp cumin, coriander
- 1/2 tsp cinnamon, ginger
- 1/4 teaspoon cayenne pepper
- 4 cups pumpkin puree, salt & pepper
- 4 cups chicken or vegetable broth
- 1/2 cup coconut milk
- Fresh cilantro, chopped, for garnish

Moroccan Spiced Pumpkin Soup

 10 mins 25 min 4

O1 Heat olive oil in a pot over medium heat. Cook onion and garlic for 5 minutes until softened.

O2 Stir in cumin, coriander, cinnamon, ginger, and cayenne (if using). Cook for 2 minutes until fragrant. Add pumpkin puree and broth, stirring to combine. Bring to a boil, reduce heat, and simmer for 15 minutes.

O3 Stir in coconut milk, season with salt and pepper, and simmer for an additional 5 minutes. Serve hot, garnished with fresh cilantro.

NUTRITIONAL VALUE

220 calories, 4g protein, 15g carbohydrates, 16g fat, 4g fiber, 0mg cholesterol, 600mg sodium, 400mg potassium.

Cretan Goat Cheese and Olive Soup

🕐 10 mins   🍲 20 min   👤 4

01 Heat olive oil in a large pot over medium heat. Cook chopped onion and minced garlic for about 5 minutes until softened.

02 Pour in chicken or vegetable broth and bring to a boil. Reduce heat and simmer for 10 minutes. Stir in heavy cream and crumbled goat cheese, whisking until melted and smooth.

03 Add sliced Kalamata olives and dried oregano. Season with salt and black pepper to taste. Simmer for an additional 5 minutes. Serve hot, garnished with fresh thyme.

INGREDIENTS

- 2 tbsp olive oil, 1 onion, chopped
- 2 cloves garlic, minced
- 4 cups chicken or vegetable broth
- 1/2 cup heavy cream, salt & pepper, 1 cup crumbled goat cheese, 1/2 cup pitted Kalamata olives, sliced, 1 tsp dried oregano
- Fresh thyme, chopped, for garnish

NUTRITIONAL VALUE

250 calories, 8g protein, 6g carbohydrates, 22g fat, 1g fiber, 40mg cholesterol, 800mg sodium, 400mg potassium.

Caldo Verde with Chorizo and Radishes

🕐 15 mins   🍲 30 min   👤 4

01 Heat olive oil in a large pot over medium heat. Cook chopped onion and minced garlic for about 5 minutes until softened.

02 Add sliced chorizo and cook until browned, about 5 minutes. Pour in chicken broth and water, bringing to a boil. Reduce heat and simmer for 10 minutes.

03 Add sliced kale and radishes to the pot. Simmer for another 10-15 minutes until the kale is tender. Season with salt and black pepper to taste. Serve hot.

INGREDIENTS

- 2 tablespoons olive oil
- 1 small onion, finely chopped
- 2 cloves garlic, minced
- 6 ounces keto-friendly chorizo, sliced, 4 cups chicken broth
- 1 cup water, 1 bunch kale, stems removed and leaves thinly sliced
- 1 cup radishes, thinly sliced
- Salt and black pepper, to taste

NUTRITIONAL VALUE

280 calories, 18g protein, 7g carbohydrates, 20g fat, 3g fiber, 50mg cholesterol, 850mg sodium, 600mg potassium.

INGREDIENTS

- 2 tbsp olive oil, I onion, chopped
- 2 cloves garlic, minced
- 4 medium zucchinis, chopped
- 4 cups chicken or vegetable broth
- 1/2 cup grated Pecorino cheese
- 1/2 cup heavy cream
- Salt and black pepper, to taste
- Fresh basil, chopped, for garnish

Italian Zucchini and Pecorino Soup

 10 mins   20 min   4

01 Heat olive oil in a large pot over medium heat. Cook chopped onion and minced garlic for about 5 minutes until softened.

02 Add chopped zucchinis and cook for another 5 minutes, stirring occasionally. Pour in broth and bring to a boil. Reduce heat and simmer for 10 minutes until zucchinis are tender.

03 Use an immersion blender to puree the soup until smooth. Stir in grated Pecorino cheese and heavy cream. Season with salt and black pepper to taste. Serve hot, garnished with fresh basil.

NUTRITIONAL VALUE	250 calories, 6g protein, 8g carbohydrates, 20g fat, 2g fiber, 40mg cholesterol, 700mg sodium, 500mg potassium.

INGREDIENTS

- 1 large head of cauliflower, cut into florets. 1 whole garlic bulb
- 3 tablespoons olive oil, divided
- 1 small onion, finely chopped
- 4 cups chicken or vegetable broth
- 1/2 cup heavy cream
- 1 tsp ground cumin, salt and pepper
- Fresh parsley, chopped, for garnish

Egyptian Roasted Garlic and Cauliflower Soup

 10 mins   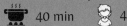 40 min   4

01 Preheat oven to 400°F (200°C). Toss cauliflower with 2 tbsp olive oil and spread on a baking sheet. Cut top off garlic, drizzle with 1 tbsp olive oil, wrap in foil, and add to sheet. Roast for 25-30 minutes.

02 Heat 1 tbsp olive oil in a pot over medium heat. Cook onion for 5 minutes. Add roasted garlic, cauliflower, and broth. Bring to a boil, then simmer for 10 minutes.

03 Puree soup. Stir in heavy cream and cumin. Season with salt and pepper. Simmer for 5 minutes. Serve hot, garnished with parsley.

NUTRITIONAL VALUE	220 calories, 4g protein, 10g carbohydrates, 18g fat, 3g fiber, 40mg cholesterol, 700mg sodium, 500mg potassium.

Macedonian Eggplant and Tomato Soup

🕐 15 mins   🍲 30 min   👤 4

INGREDIENTS

- 2 tbsp olive oil, I large eggplant, diced6 I small onion, finely chopped
- 2 cloves garlic, minced
- 4 large tomatoes, chopped
- 4 cups vegetable broth
- I tsp dried oregano, I tsp paprika
- Salt and black pepper, to taste
- Fresh basil, chopped, for garnish

O1   Heat olive oil in a pot over medium heat. Cook diced eggplant until slightly browned, about 5-7 minutes. Remove and set aside.

O2   In the same pot, cook chopped onion and minced garlic for 5 minutes until softened. Add chopped tomatoes, cooked eggplant, vegetable broth, oregano, and paprika. Bring to a boil, then simmer for 20 minutes.

O3   Puree the soup to desired consistency with an immersion blender. Season with salt and pepper. Serve hot, garnished with fresh basil.

NUTRITIONAL VALUE

180 calories, 4g protein, 12g carbohydrates, 14g fat, 4g fiber, 0mg cholesterol, 650mg sodium, 500mg potassium.

Lebanese Lentil Soup (Low Carb Version)

🕐 10 mins   🍲 30 min   👤 4

INGREDIENTS

- 2 tablespoons olive oil
- I small onion, finely chopped
- 2 cloves garlic, minced
- I cup cauliflower rice
- 1/2 cup red lentils, rinsed
- 4 cups vegetable broth
- I tsp cumin, coriander
- 1/2 teaspoon ground turmeric
- Salt and black pepper, to taste
- Fresh cilantro, chopped, for garnish
- Fresh lemon wedges, for serving

O1   Heat olive oil in a pot over medium heat. Cook chopped onion and minced garlic for 5 minutes until softened.

O2   Add cauliflower rice, rinsed red lentils, vegetable broth, cumin, coriander, and turmeric. Bring to a boil, then simmer for 20-25 minutes until tender.

O3   Puree the soup until smooth with an immersion blender. Season with salt and pepper. Serve hot, garnished with fresh cilantro and a squeeze of lemon juice.

NUTRITIONAL VALUE

200 calories, 8g protein, 14g carbohydrates, 10g fat, 6g fiber, 0mg cholesterol, 600mg sodium, 500mg potassium.

INGREDIENTS

- I whole rabbit, cut into pieces
- 2 tbsp olive oil, I onion, chopped
- 2 cloves garlic, minced
- 2 carrots, chopped, 2 celery stalks, chopped, I zucchini, chopped
- 4 cups chicken broth
- 2 cups water, I tsp dried thyme
- I teaspoon dried rosemary
- Salt and black pepper, to taste
- Fresh parsley, chopped, for garnish

Maltese Rabbit and Vegetable Broth

 15 mins   45 min   4

01 Heat olive oil in a pot over medium heat. Brown rabbit pieces on all sides for 5-7 minutes. Remove and set aside. In the same pot, sauté chopped onion and minced garlic for 5 minutes. Add chopped carrots, celery, and zucchini, cooking for another 5 minutes.

02 Return rabbit to the pot. Add chicken broth, water, thyme, and rosemary. Bring to a boil, then simmer for 30 minutes until rabbit and vegetables are tender.

03 Season with salt and pepper. Serve hot, garnished with fresh parsley.

NUTRITIONAL VALUE	300 calories, 25g protein, 10g carbohydrates, 18g fat, 3g fiber, 90mg cholesterol, 600mg sodium, 700mg potassium.

INGREDIENTS

- 2 large avocados, peeled and pitted
- 2 large cucumbers, peeled and chopped, I cup full-fat Greek yogurt
- I cup cold water
- 2 cloves garlic, minced
- 2 tablespoons fresh lemon juice
- 1/4 cup fresh dill, chopped
- Salt and black pepper, to taste
- Fresh dill, for garnish

Israeli Avocado and Cucumber Cold Soup

 15 mins   0 min   4

01 In a blender, combine avocados, cucumbers, Greek yogurt, cold water, minced garlic, lemon juice, and chopped dill. Blend until smooth.

02 Season with salt and black pepper to taste. Adjust consistency with more water if necessary. Chill the soup in the refrigerator for at least I hour before serving.

03 Serve cold, garnished with fresh dill.

NUTRITIONAL VALUE	220 calories, 4g protein, 12g carbohydrates, 18g fat, 7g fiber, 10mg cholesterol, 200mg sodium, 600mg potassium.

SALADS

INGREDIENTS

- 2 cups full-fat Greek yogurt
- 2 large cucumbers, diced
- 2 cloves garlic, minced
- 2 tablespoons fresh dill, chopped
- I tablespoon fresh mint, chopped
- 2 tablespoons olive oil
- Juice of I lemon
- Salt and black pepper, to taste

Turkish Cucumber and Yogurt Salad (Cacık)

🕐 10 mins   🍲 0 min   👤 4

O1 In a large bowl, combine Greek yogurt, minced garlic, chopped dill, and chopped mint.

O2 Add diced cucumbers to the yogurt mixture and stir to combine. Drizzle with olive oil and lemon juice. Season with salt and black pepper to taste.

O3 Mix well and chill in the refrigerator for at least 30 minutes. Serve cold, garnished with additional fresh herbs if desired.

NUTRITIONAL VALUE

120 calories, 6g protein, 8g carbohydrates, 8g fat, 1g fiber, 10mg cholesterol, 200mg sodium, 250mg potassium.

INGREDIENTS

- 4 ounces chorizo sausage, sliced
- 2 large red bell peppers, roasted and sliced, I cup cherry tomatoes, halved
- 1/4 cup red onion, thinly sliced
- 1/4 cup black olives, pitted and sliced
- 2 tablespoons fresh parsley, chopped
- 2 tablespoons olive oil
- I tablespoon red wine vinegar
- Salt and black pepper, to taste

Spanish Chorizo and Roasted Pepper Salad

🕐 15 mins   🍲 10 min   👤 4

O1 Cook sliced chorizo in a skillet over medium heat for 5-7 minutes until browned. Set aside.

O2 In a large bowl, combine roasted red peppers, cherry tomatoes, red onion, black olives, and parsley. Add cooked chorizo.

O3 Whisk olive oil and red wine vinegar in a small bowl. Season with salt and pepper. Pour over the salad, toss gently, and serve immediately.

NUTRITIONAL VALUE

250 calories, 12g protein, 8g carbohydrates, 18g fat, 3g fiber, 35mg cholesterol, 700mg sodium, 300mg potassium.

Turkish Roasted Eggplant and Yogurt Salad

🕐 15 mins   🍲 25 min   👤 4

01 Preheat oven to 400°F (200°C). Halve and score eggplants, brush with olive oil, and season. Roast cut side down for 25 minutes. Cool slightly, then chop finely.

02 Mix Greek yogurt, minced garlic, lemon juice, dill, parsley, tahini, and smoked paprika in a bowl. Add chopped eggplant and mix well. Adjust seasoning.

03 Chill for 15 minutes. Serve chilled or at room temperature, garnished with fresh herbs if desired.

NUTRITIONAL VALUE

130 calories, 5g protein, 12g carbohydrates, 7g fat, 5g fiber, 5mg cholesterol, 180mg sodium, 400mg potassium.

INGREDIENTS

- 2 large eggplants, 1 tbsp olive oil
- Salt and pepper, to taste
- 1 cup plain Greek yogurt
- 2 cloves garlic, minced
- 1 tablespoon lemon juice
- 2 tbsp fresh dill, chopped
- 2 tbsp fresh parsley, chopped
- 1 tbsp tahini (optional)
- 1 tsp smoked paprika (optional)

Lebanese Fattoush Salad (Keto Version)

🕐 15 mins   🍲 0 min   👤 4

01 In a large bowl, combine romaine lettuce, cherry tomatoes, cucumber, red bell pepper, radishes, red onion, parsley, and mint.

02 In a small bowl, whisk together olive oil, lemon juice, ground sumac, salt, and black pepper. Pour the dressing over the salad and toss gently to combine.

03 Top with crumbled feta cheese and sliced almonds or keto-friendly croutons if desired. Serve immediately.

NUTRITIONAL VALUE

180 calories, 3g protein, 8g carbohydrates, 16g fat, 3g fiber, 10mg cholesterol, 220mg sodium, 350mg potassium.

INGREDIENTS

- 2 cups romaine lettuce, chopped
- 1 cup cherry tomatoes, halved
- 1 large cucumber, diced
- 1/2 red bell pepper, chopped
- 1/4 cup radishes, thinly sliced
- 1/4 red onion, thinly sliced
- 1/4 cup parsley, mint, chopped
- 1/4 cup olive oil, 2 tbsp lemon juice
- 1 tsp ground sumac, salt and pepper
- 1/2 cup crumbled feta cheese
- 1/2 cup sliced almonds or keto-friendly croutons (optional)

INGREDIENTS

- 4 large carrots, peeled and sliced
- 2 tbsp olive oil
- 1 tsp cumin, 1 tsp coriander
- 1/2 tsp cinnamon, salt and pepper
- 2 ripe avocados, diced
- 1/4 cup fresh cilantro, chopped
- 1/4 cup fresh parsley, chopped
- 1 tbsp lemon juice
- 1 tbsp tahini, 2 tbsp pumpkin seeds

Moroccan Roasted Carrot and Avocado Salad

 15 mins 25 min 👤 4

O1 Preheat the oven to 400°F (200°C). Toss sliced carrots with olive oil, cumin, coriander, cinnamon, salt, and pepper. Spread on a baking sheet and roast for 25 minutes until tender and caramelized.

O2 In a large bowl, combine roasted carrots, diced avocados, cilantro, parsley, lemon juice, and tahini. Mix gently to combine. Adjust seasoning with salt and pepper, and sprinkle with pumpkin seeds if using.

O3 Chill in the refrigerator for at least 15 minutes before serving. Serve chilled or at room temperature.

NUTRITIONAL VALUE	220 calories, 3g protein, 18g carbohydrates, 16g fat, 8g fiber, 0mg cholesterol, 240mg sodium, 720mg potassium.

INGREDIENTS

- 1 pound shrimp, peeled and deveined
- 2 tbsp olive oil, 2 ripe avocados, diced
- 1 cup cherry tomatoes, halved
- 1/4 cup red onion, finely chopped
- 1/4 cup fresh parsley, chopped
- 1/4 cup fresh lemon juice
- Salt and black pepper, to taste
- Lemon wedges, for serving

Croatian Shrimp and Avocado Salad

 15 mins 🍲 5 min 👤 4

O1 Heat olive oil in a skillet over medium heat. Cook shrimp for 2-3 minutes on each side until pink and opaque. Remove and let cool slightly.

O2 In a large bowl, combine diced avocados, cherry tomatoes, red onion, and fresh parsley. Add cooked shrimp.

O3 Drizzle with lemon juice and season with salt and pepper. Toss gently to combine. Serve immediately with lemon wedges on the side.

NUTRITIONAL VALUE	300 calories, 22g protein, 10g carbohydrates, 20g fat, 7g fiber, 180mg cholesterol, 350mg sodium, 600mg potassium.

Egyptian Eggplant and Nut Salad

🕐 15 mins   🍲 20 min   👤 4

INGREDIENTS

- 2 medium eggplants, diced
- 1/4 cup olive oil, divided
- 1/2 cup walnuts, chopped
- 1/2 cup almonds, chopped
- 1/4 cup pine nuts, salt and pepper
- 1/4 cup fresh parsley, chopped
- 1/4 cup fresh mint, chopped
- 1/4 cup lemon juice
- 2 cloves garlic, minced

01 Preheat oven to 400°F (200°C). Toss diced eggplant with 2 tbsp olive oil and roast for 20 minutes until tender and golden. Let cool. Toast walnuts, almonds, and pine nuts in a dry skillet over medium heat for 3-5 minutes. Cool.

02 Combine roasted eggplant, toasted nuts, parsley, and mint in a large bowl. Whisk together remaining olive oil, lemon juice, garlic, salt, and pepper in a small bowl. Pour over salad and toss gently.

03 Serve immediately or chill for 30 minutes before serving.

NUTRITIONAL VALUE

280 calories, 6g protein, 12g carbohydrates, 24g fat, 6g fiber, 0mg cholesterol, 150mg sodium, 500mg potassium.

Cypriot Halloumi and Mint Salad

🕐 10 mins   🍲 10 min   👤 4

INGREDIENTS

- 8 ounces halloumi cheese, sliced
- 2 tablespoons olive oil
- 2 cups mixed salad greens
- 1 cup cherry tomatoes, halved
- 1/2 cucumber, sliced
- 1/4 cup red onion, thinly sliced
- 1/4 cup fresh mint leaves, chopped
- 2 tablespoons fresh lemon juice
- Salt and black pepper, to taste

01 Heat olive oil in a skillet over medium heat. Cook halloumi slices until golden brown, about 2-3 minutes per side. Remove and let cool slightly.

02 In a large bowl, combine mixed salad greens, cherry tomatoes, cucumber, red onion, and fresh mint leaves. In a small bowl, whisk together lemon juice, salt, and black pepper. Pour dressing over the salad and toss gently.

03 Top the salad with warm halloumi slices. Serve immediately.

NUTRITIONAL VALUE

250 calories, 12g protein, 8g carbohydrates, 20g fat, 2g fiber, 40mg cholesterol, 800mg sodium, 300mg potassium.

INGREDIENTS

- 4 medium beetroots, roasted and sliced, salt and pepper
- 4 oz goat cheese, crumbled
- 1/4 cup walnuts, toasted and chopped
- 2 tablespoons fresh mint, chopped
- 2 tablespoons fresh parsley, chopped
- 2 tablespoons olive oil
- 1 tablespoon balsamic vinegar

Albanian Beetroot and Goat Cheese Salad

🕐 20 mins 🍲 30 min 👤 4

01 Preheat the oven to 400°F (200°C). Wrap beetroots in foil and roast for 30 minutes until tender. Allow to cool, then peel and slice.

02 In a large bowl, combine sliced beetroots, crumbled goat cheese, toasted walnuts, mint, and parsley. In a small bowl, whisk together olive oil, balsamic vinegar, salt, and pepper. Pour the dressing over the salad and toss gently.

03 Adjust seasoning with additional salt and pepper if needed. Serve chilled or at room temperature.

NUTRITIONAL VALUE	250 calories, 7g protein, 18g carbohydrates, 18g fat, 5g fiber, 15mg cholesterol, 200mg sodium, 400mg potassium.

INGREDIENTS

- 2 ripe avocados, diced
- 2 tomatoes, diced
- 1/2 red onion, finely chopped
- 1/4 cup fresh parsley, chopped
- 2 tablespoons olive oil
- 1 tablespoon fresh lemon juice
- 1 teaspoon za'atar spice blend
- Salt and black pepper, to taste

Israeli Avocado and Tomato Salad with Za'atar

🕐 10 mins 🍲 0 min 👤 4

01 In a large bowl, combine diced avocados, diced tomatoes, and finely chopped red onion. Add chopped parsley to the bowl.

02 In a small bowl, whisk together olive oil, lemon juice, za'atar, salt, and black pepper. Pour the dressing over the avocado and tomato mixture and toss gently.

03 Serve immediately.

NUTRITIONAL VALUE	250 calories, 3g protein, 12g carbohydrates, 22g fat, 7g fiber, 0mg cholesterol, 200mg sodium, 600mg potassium.

Maltese Tomato and Asparagus Salad

 15 mins — 20 min — 4

01 Blanch the asparagus in boiling water for 2-3 minutes until tender-crisp. Drain and rinse with cold water to stop the cooking process.

02 In a large bowl, combine the asparagus, sun-dried tomatoes, Kalamata olives, and crumbled feta cheese. In a small bowl, whisk together olive oil, red wine vinegar, minced garlic, salt, and pepper.

03 Pour the dressing over the salad and toss to combine. Serve immediately or refrigerate for 15 minutes to allow flavors to meld. Garnish with green onions.

INGREDIENTS

- 1 bunch asparagus, trimmed and cut into bite-sized pieces
- 1/4 cup sun-dried tomatoes, chopped, 1/4 cup Kalamata olives
- 1/4 cup crumbled feta cheese
- 2 tablespoons extra virgin olive oil
- 1 tablespoon red wine vinegar
- 1 clove garlic, minced, salt and pepper, chopped green onions to garnish

NUTRITIONAL VALUE

150 calories, 4g protein, 6g carbohydrates, 12g fat, 3g fiber, 10mg cholesterol, 200mg sodium, 250mg potassium.

Spinach and Strawberry Salad with Walnuts

 10 mins 0 min 4

01 In a large bowl, combine fresh spinach, sliced strawberries, red onion, toasted walnuts, and crumbled feta cheese.

02 In a small bowl, whisk together olive oil, balsamic vinegar, salt, and black pepper.

03 Pour the dressing over the salad and toss gently to combine. Serve immediately.

INGREDIENTS

- 4 cups fresh spinach, washed and dried, 3 tbsp olive oil
- 1 cup strawberries, hulled and sliced, 1/4 cup red onion, thinly sliced, 1/2 cup walnuts, toasted
- 1/4 cup feta cheese, crumbled
- 2 tablespoons balsamic vinegar
- Salt and black pepper, to taste

NUTRITIONAL VALUE

200 calories, 4g protein, 12g carbohydrates, 16g fat, 3g fiber, 10mg cholesterol, 200mg sodium, 400mg potassium.

INGREDIENTS

- 4 large tomatoes, sliced
- 8 ounces fresh mozzarella, sliced
- 1/4 cup fresh basil leaves
- 1 cup fresh basil leaves
- 1/4 cup pine nuts
- 1/2 cup grated Parmesan cheese
- 1/2 cup olive oil, 2 cloves garlic, minced, salt and pepper

Italian Caprese Salad with Keto Pesto

 10 mins 0 min 4

O1 In a food processor, combine basil leaves, pine nuts, grated Parmesan, minced garlic, salt, and black pepper. Pulse until finely chopped. With the processor running, slowly add olive oil until smooth and well combined.

O2 Arrange tomato and mozzarella slices on a serving platter, alternating between each slice. Tuck fresh basil leaves between the tomato and mozzarella slices.

O3 Drizzle the keto pesto over the tomato and mozzarella. Serve immediately.

NUTRITIONAL VALUE	320 calories, 12g protein, 5g carbohydrates, 28g fat, 2g fiber, 30mg cholesterol, 350mg sodium, 400mg potassium.

INGREDIENTS

- 4 cups kale, chopped
- 1 cup low-carb chickpeas (use chickpeas with lower net carbs)
- 1/2 cup cherry tomatoes, halved
- 1/4 cup red onion, thinly sliced
- 1/4 cup Kalamata olives, pitted and halved, 1/4 cup olive oil
- 1/4 cup feta cheese, crumbled
- 2 tbsp lemon juice, 1 tsp oregano
- Salt and black pepper, to taste

Mediterranean Kale and Chickpea Salad

 15 mins 0 min 4

O1 In a large bowl, combine chopped kale, low-carb chickpeas, cherry tomatoes, red onion, Kalamata olives, and crumbled feta cheese.

O2 In a small bowl, whisk together olive oil, lemon juice, dried oregano, salt, and black pepper.

O3 Pour the dressing over the salad and toss gently to combine. Serve immediately.

NUTRITIONAL VALUE	250 calories, 8g protein, 12g carbohydrates, 18g fat, 6g fiber, 15mg cholesterol, 350mg sodium, 500mg potassium.

Albanian Cucumber and Olive Salad

🕐 10 mins　　🍲 0 min　　👤 4

O1　In a large bowl, combine cucumbers, Kalamata olives, red onion, and fresh dill.

O2　In a small bowl, whisk together olive oil, red wine vinegar, salt, and black pepper.

O3　Pour the dressing over the salad and toss gently to combine. Top with crumbled feta cheese. Serve immediately.

INGREDIENTS

- 2 large cucumbers, sliced
- 1/2 cup Kalamata olives, pitted
- 1/4 cup red onion, thinly sliced
- 1/4 cup fresh dill, chopped
- 1/4 cup feta cheese, crumbled
- 3 tablespoons olive oil
- 2 tablespoons red wine vinegar
- Salt and black pepper, to taste

NUTRITIONAL VALUE	180 calories, 3g protein, 8g carbohydrates, 16g fat, 2g fiber, 10mg cholesterol, 350mg sodium, 300mg potassium.

Venetian Radicchio and Goat Cheese Salad

🕐 10 mins　　🍲 0 min　　👤 4

O1　In a large bowl, combine chopped radicchio, mixed salad greens, cherry tomatoes, red onion, and toasted walnuts.

O2　In a small bowl, whisk together olive oil, balsamic vinegar, salt, and black pepper.

O3　Pour the dressing over the salad and toss gently to combine. Top with crumbled goat cheese. Serve immediately.

INGREDIENTS

- 2 cups radicchio, chopped
- 2 cups mixed salad greens
- 1/2 cup cherry tomatoes, halved
- 1/4 cup red onion, thinly sliced
- 1/4 cup walnuts, toasted and chopped, 4 ounces goat cheese, crumbled, 3 tablespoons olive oil
- 2 tablespoons balsamic vinegar
- Salt and black pepper, to taste

NUTRITIONAL VALUE	220 calories, 6g protein, 8g carbohydrates, 18g fat, 3g fiber, 10mg cholesterol, 250mg sodium, 400mg potassium.

INGREDIENTS

- 2 cups cherry tomatoes, halved
- I large cucumber, diced
- I red bell pepper, chopped
- I small red onion, thinly sliced
- 1/2 cup Kalamata olives, pitted
- I cup crumbled feta cheese
- Fresh parsley, chopped, for garnish
- 1/4 cup full-fat Greek yogurt
- 1/4 cup olive oil, 2 tbsp lemon juice
- I clove garlic, minced

Greek Village Salad with Creamy Feta Dressing

 15 mins 0 min 4

O1 In a large bowl, combine the cherry tomatoes, cucumber, red bell pepper, red onion, and Kalamata olives. Toss gently to mix.

O2 In a blender or food processor, combine the crumbled feta cheese, Greek yogurt, olive oil, lemon juice, minced garlic, salt, and black pepper. Blend until smooth and creamy.

O3 Pour the creamy feta dressing over the salad and toss gently to coat all the ingredients. Garnish with additional crumbled feta cheese and fresh parsley. Serve immediately.

NUTRITIONAL VALUE	220 calories, 5g protein, 10g carbohydrates, 18g fat, 3g fiber, 25mg cholesterol, 400mg sodium, 350mg potassium.

INGREDIENTS

- 2 cups romaine lettuce, chopped
- I cup cherry tomatoes, halved
- I cup cucumber, diced
- 1/2 cup Kalamata olives, pitted and halved, 1/4 cup red onion, thinly sliced
- 4 ounces salami, sliced
- 4 ounces provolone cheese, cubed
- 1/4 cup grated Parmesan cheese
- 1/4 cup extra virgin olive oil
- 2 tbsp red wine vinegar, I tsp oregano
- Salt and black pepper, to taste

Antipasto Salad with Salami and Provolone

 15 mins 0 min 4

O1 In a large salad bowl, combine chopped romaine lettuce, cherry tomatoes, cucumber, Kalamata olives, and red onion. Add sliced salami and cubed provolone cheese to the salad.

O2 In a small bowl, whisk together extra virgin olive oil, red wine vinegar, dried oregano, salt, and black pepper. Pour the dressing over the salad and toss gently to combine all ingredients.

O3 Sprinkle grated Parmesan cheese over the top and serve immediately.

NUTRITIONAL VALUE	320 calories, 14g protein, 8g carbohydrates, 26g fat, 3g fiber, 45mg cholesterol, 900mg sodium, 400mg potassium.

SIDE DISHES

INGREDIENTS

- 4 medium zucchinis, spiralized
- 1/2 cup sundried tomatoes, chopped
- 1/2 cup feta cheese, crumbled
- 1/4 cup Kalamata olives, pitted and halved, 2 tablespoons olive oil
- 2 cloves garlic, minced
- 1 tablespoon fresh lemon juice
- 1 teaspoon dried oregano
- Salt and black pepper, to taste
- Fresh basil, chopped, for garnish

Zucchini Noodles with Feta and Dried Tomatoes

 10 mins   10 min   4

O1 Heat olive oil in a large skillet over medium heat. Add minced garlic and cook for 1 minute until fragrant.

O2 Add spiralized zucchini noodles and sauté for 2-3 minutes until just tender. Stir in sundried tomatoes, Kalamata olives, lemon juice, and dried oregano. Cook for an additional 2 minutes.

O3 Remove from heat and toss with crumbled feta cheese. Season with salt and black pepper. Garnish with fresh basil and serve immediately.

NUTRITIONAL VALUE

220 calories, 6g protein, 12g carbohydrates, 16g fat, 4g fiber, 20mg cholesterol, 400mg sodium, 600mg potassium.

INGREDIENTS

- 2 medium eggplants, sliced into 1/2inch rounds, 2 tablespoons olive oil
- 1 cup marinara sauce (sugar free)
- 1 1/2 cups shredded mozzarella cheese
- 1/2 cup grated Parmesan cheese
- 1/4 cup almond flour
- 1 tsp oregano, basil, salt and pepper
- Salt and black pepper, to taste

Italian Eggplant Parmesan Stacks

 20 mins   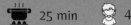 25 min   4

O1 Preheat oven to 375°F (190°C). Line a baking sheet with parchment. Brush eggplant slices with olive oil, season, and bake for 15 minutes, flipping halfway.

O2 Mix almond flour, Parmesan, oregano, and basil. Remove eggplant, spread with marinara, sprinkle with almond mixture, and top with mozzarella.

O3 Stack slices with sauce and cheese. Bake 10 minutes until bubbly. Garnish with basil and serve immediately.

NUTRITIONAL VALUE

320 calories, 18g protein, 10g carbohydrates, 24g fat, 6g fiber, 50mg cholesterol, 600mg sodium, 400mg potassium.

Turkish Spiced Spinach with Yogurt

🕐 10 mins   🍲 15 min   🧑 4

O1   Heat olive oil in a skillet over medium heat. Sauté chopped onion until translucent, about 5 minutes.

O2   Add minced garlic, cumin, paprika, cinnamon, and nutmeg. Cook for 1-2 minutes, stirring until fragrant. Add chopped spinach and cook until wilted about 5 minutes. Season with salt and pepper.

O3   Remove from heat, let cool slightly, then stir in Greek yogurt. Serve immediately, drizzled with fresh lemon juice.

INGREDIENTS

- 2 tablespoons olive oil
- 1 large onion, finely chopped
- 2 cloves garlic, minced
- 1 tsp cumin, paprika
- 1/2 tsp cinnamon, nutmeg
- 1 pound fresh spinach, washed and chopped, 1 cup full-fat Greek yogurt
- Salt and black pepper, to taste
- Fresh lemon juice, to taste

NUTRITIONAL VALUE

150 calories, 5g protein, 10g carbohydrates, 10g fat, 3g fiber, 10mg cholesterol, 200mg sodium, 700mg potassium.

Lebanese Lemon Garlic Cauliflower Mash

🕐 10 mins   🍲 15 min   🧑 4

O1   Bring a large pot of salted water to a boil. Add cauliflower florets and cook until tender, about 10 minutes. Drain well.

O2   In the same pot, heat olive oil over medium heat. Add minced garlic and cook until fragrant, about 1-2 minutes. Add cooked cauliflower back to the pot.

O3   Using an immersion blender or potato masher, blend or mash cauliflower until smooth and creamy. Stir in fresh lemon juice, chopped parsley, salt, and black pepper. Mix well. Serve immediately.

INGREDIENTS

- 1 large head of cauliflower, cut into florets
- 2 tablespoons olive oil
- 3 cloves garlic, minced
- 1/4 cup fresh lemon juice
- 1/4 cup fresh parsley, chopped
- Salt and black pepper, to taste

NUTRITIONAL VALUE

110 calories, 3g protein, 10g carbohydrates, 7g fat, 4g fiber, 0mg cholesterol, 200mg sodium, 350mg potassium.

INGREDIENTS

- 1 lb Brussels sprouts, trimmed and halved
- 4 oz chorizo sausage, sliced
- 2 tablespoons olive oil
- 1 teaspoon smoked paprika
- Salt and pepper, to taste
- 1 tablespoon fresh parsley, chopped

Portuguese Chorizo Roasted Brussels Sprouts

🕐 10 mins 25 min 👤 4

O1   Preheat the oven to 400°F (200°C).

O2   In a large bowl, toss the Brussels sprouts with olive oil, smoked paprika, salt, and pepper. Spread the Brussels sprouts on a baking sheet and scatter the chorizo slices over them.

O3   Roast in the oven for 20-25 minutes, until Brussels sprouts are tender and chorizo is crispy. Sprinkle with chopped parsley before serving, if desired.

NUTRITIONAL VALUE

220 calories, 10g protein, 10g carbohydrates, 17g fat, 4g fiber, 25mg cholesterol, 480mg sodium, 450mg potassium.

INGREDIENTS

- 1 lb mushrooms, cleaned and halved
- 3 tablespoons olive oil
- 2 tablespoons lemon juice
- 2 cloves garlic, minced
- 1 teaspoon dried oregano
- 1 teaspoon dried thyme
- Salt and pepper, to taste
- 1 tablespoon fresh parsley, chopped

Italian Lemon and Herb Roasted Mushrooms

🕐 10 mins 20 min 👤 4

O1   Preheat the oven to 400°F (200°C).

O2   In a large bowl, combine the olive oil, lemon juice, garlic, oregano, thyme, salt, and pepper. Add the mushrooms and toss to coat.

O3   Spread the mushrooms in a single layer on a baking sheet. Roast in the preheated oven for 15-20 minutes, until the mushrooms are tender and golden brown. Sprinkle with chopped parsley before serving, if desired.

NUTRITIONAL VALUE

120 calories, 2g protein, 6g carbohydrates, 10g fat, 2g fiber, 0mg cholesterol, 5mg sodium, 300mg potassium.

Baked Radishes with Kalamata Olives

 10 mins   🍲 25 min   👤 4

O1 Preheat the oven to 400°F (200°C).

O2 In a large bowl, toss radishes and Kalamata olives with olive oil, dried oregano, garlic powder, salt, and black pepper until well coated. Spread the mixture on a baking sheet in a single layer.

O3 Bake for 20-25 minutes until radishes are tender and lightly browned. Remove from the oven, transfer to a serving dish, and sprinkle with crumbled feta cheese and fresh parsley. Serve immediately.

NUTRITIONAL VALUE

150 calories, 3g protein, 6g carbohydrates, 12g fat, 2g fiber, 10mg cholesterol, 400mg sodium, 300mg potassium.

INGREDIENTS

- 1 pound radishes, trimmed and halved
- 1/4 cup Kalamata olives, pitted and halved
- 3 tablespoons olive oil
- 1 teaspoon dried oregano
- 1 teaspoon garlic powder
- 1/2 teaspoon salt
- 1/4 teaspoon black pepper
- 1/4 cup crumbled feta cheese
- 1 tablespoon fresh parsley, chopped

Egyptian Spiced Green Beans with Tomato

 10 mins   🍲 20 min   4

O1 Heat olive oil in a skillet over medium heat. Sauté chopped onion for 5 minutes. Add garlic, cumin, coriander, cinnamon, and cayenne. Cook for 1-2 minutes.

O2 Add green beans and tomato, stirring to coat with spices. Season with salt and pepper. Cover and cook for 15-20 minutes, stirring occasionally, until beans are tender.

O3 Sprinkle with fresh parsley before serving.

NUTRITIONAL VALUE

110 calories, 2g protein, 10g carbohydrates, 7g fat, 4g fiber, 0mg cholesterol, 150mg sodium, 350mg potassium.

INGREDIENTS

- 1 lb green beans, trimmed
- 2 tbsp olive oil, 1 onion, chopped
- 3 cloves garlic, minced
- 1 tsp cumin, coriander
- 1/2 tsp cinnamon, salt and pepper
- 1/4 tsp cayenne pepper (optional)
- 1 large tomato, chopped
- 2 tbsp fresh parsley, chopped

INGREDIENTS

- 1 lb carrots, peeled and cut into sticks
- 2 tablespoons olive oil
- 1 teaspoon ground cinnamon
- 1 teaspoon ground cumin
- 1 tablespoon honey (optional, adjust for keto preferences)
- Salt and pepper, to taste
- 1 tablespoon fresh parsley, chopped (optional)

Moroccan Cinnamon Roasted Carrots

🕐 10 mins   🍲 25 min   👤 4

01   Preheat the oven to 400°F (200°C).

02   In a large bowl, combine olive oil, cinnamon, cumin, honey (if using), salt, and pepper. Add the carrot sticks and toss to coat. Spread the carrots in a single layer on a baking sheet.

03   Roast for 20-25 minutes until tender and slightly caramelized. Sprinkle with chopped parsley before serving, if desired.

NUTRITIONAL VALUE	110 calories, 1g protein, 10g carbohydrates, 7g fat, 3g fiber, 0mg cholesterol, 200mg sodium, 320mg potassium.

INGREDIENTS

- 1 large head of cauliflower, cut into florets, 1/4 cup tahini
- 2 tablespoons olive oil
- 2 cloves garlic, minced
- 1/4 cup lemon juice
- 1 teaspoon ground cumin
- 1 teaspoon paprika
- Salt and black pepper, to taste
- 1/4 cup fresh parsley, chopped

Turkish Cauliflower and Tahini Bake

🕐 15 mins   🍲 30 min   👤 4

01   Preheat the oven to 400°F (200°C). Lightly grease a baking dish with olive oil.

02   In a large bowl, combine tahini, olive oil, minced garlic, lemon juice, ground cumin, paprika, salt, and black pepper. Mix well. Add cauliflower florets to the bowl and toss to coat evenly.

03   Transfer coated cauliflower to the baking dish and spread in an even layer. Bake for 30 minutes, or until tender and golden brown. Sprinkle with fresh parsley before serving.

NUTRITIONAL VALUE	180 calories, 5g protein, 12g carbohydrates, 14g fat, 4g fiber, 0mg cholesterol, 250mg sodium, 450mg potassium.

Stuffed Eggplants with Pine Nuts and Spices

 20 mins   40 min 4

INGREDIENTS

- 4 small eggplants, 1/4 cup olive oil
- 1 onion, finely chopped
- 2 cloves garlic, minced
- 1/2 pound ground beef or lamb
- 1/4 cup pine nuts, toasted
- 1 tsp cinnamon, cumin
- 1/2 tsp allspice, salt and pepper
- 1/2 cup fresh parsley, chopped
- 1 cup tomato sauce (sugarfree)

O1 Preheat oven to 375°F (190°C). Halve eggplants and scoop out the flesh, leaving 1/2 inch shells. Chop flesh and set aside.

O2 Heat olive oil in a skillet over medium heat. Sauté onion and garlic for 5 minutes. Add ground meat, eggplant flesh, pine nuts, spices, salt, and pepper. Cook until browned, about 10 minutes. Stir in parsley.

O3 Stuff eggplant shells with meat mixture and place in a baking dish. Pour tomato sauce over them. Cover with foil and bake for 30 minutes. Remove foil and bake for 10 more minutes until tender. Serve immediately.

NUTRITIONAL VALUE

320 calories, 18g protein, 14g carbohydrates, 22g fat, 6g fiber, 45mg cholesterol, 400mg sodium, 700mg potassium.

Israeli Roasted Eggplant with Tahini Drizzle

 10 mins   30 min   4

INGREDIENTS

- 2 large eggplants, sliced lengthwise
- 1/4 cup olive oil, salt and pepper
- 1/2 cup tahini
- 1/4 cup lemon juice
- 2 cloves garlic, minced
- 1/4 cup water (adjust for desired consistency)
- 2 tbsp fresh parsley, chopped

O1 Preheat the oven to 400°F (200°C). Place eggplant slices on a baking sheet, brush with olive oil, and season with salt and pepper.

O2 Roast eggplants for 25-30 minutes until tender and golden brown. While roasting, prepare the tahini drizzle by whisking tahini, lemon juice, minced garlic, and water in a small bowl until smooth, adjusting water for desired consistency.

O3 Remove eggplants from oven and arrange on a serving platter. Drizzle with tahini sauce, garnish with chopped parsley, and serve immediately.

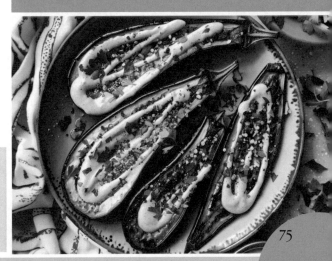

NUTRITIONAL VALUE

210 calories, 4g protein, 10g carbohydrates, 18g fat, 6g fiber, 0mg cholesterol, 150mg sodium, 500mg potassium.

INGREDIENTS

- 1 lb fresh green beans, trimmed
- 2 tablespoons olive oil
- 3 cloves garlic, minced
- Zest of 1 lemon, 2 tbsp fresh lemon juice, 1/4 tsp dried oregano
- Salt and pepper to taste
- 1/4 cup crumbled feta cheese
- Fresh parsley, chopped, for garnish

Greek Lemon Garlic Green Beans

 10 mins   15 min   4

01 Boil salted water in a large pot. Cook green beans for 3-4 minutes until tender but crisp. Drain, then cool in ice water. Drain again and set aside.

02 Heat olive oil in a skillet over medium heat. Sauté minced garlic for 1 minute. Add green beans, tossing to coat. Cook for 2-3 minutes, stirring occasionally.

03 Add lemon zest, juice, and oregano. Toss and season with salt and pepper. Cook for 2 more minutes. Transfer to a dish, sprinkle with feta, and garnish with parsley if desired.

NUTRITIONAL VALUE

120 calories, 3g protein, 10g carbohydrates, 8g fat, 4g fiber, 0mg cholesterol, 180mg sodium, 250mg potassium.

INGREDIENTS

- 2 cups canned chickpeas, drained and rinsed, 2 tablespoons olive oil
- 1 tablespoon ground sumac
- 1 teaspoon ground cumin
- 1 teaspoon paprika
- Salt, to taste
- Black pepper, to taste

Turkish Roasted Chickpeas with Sumac

 10 mins   30 min   4

01 Preheat the oven to 400°F (200°C). In a bowl, combine chickpeas, olive oil, sumac, cumin, paprika, salt, and pepper. Toss until evenly coated.

02 Spread chickpeas in a single layer on a parchment-lined baking sheet. Roast for 25-30 minutes, stirring occasionally, until crispy and golden brown.

03 Remove from the oven and let cool slightly before serving.

NUTRITIONAL VALUE

180 calories, 7g protein, 20g carbohydrates, 8g fat, 6g fiber, 0mg cholesterol, 250mg sodium, 230mg potassium.

Maliese Pea and Mint Purée

🕐 10 mins   🍲 15 min   👤 4

O1 In a pot of boiling water, cook the peas for 5-7 minutes until tender. Drain and set aside.

O2 In a skillet, heat the olive oil over medium heat. Add the onion and garlic, and sauté for 5 minutes until softened.

O3 In a blender or food processor, combine the cooked peas, sautéed onion and garlic, fresh mint, salt, pepper, and lemon juice. Blend until smooth. Adjust seasoning to taste and serve warm.

NUTRITIONAL VALUE

120 calories, 4g protein, 14g carbohydrates, 6g fat, 5g fiber, 0mg cholesterol, 210mg sodium, 240mg potassium.

INGREDIENTS

- 2 cups fresh or frozen peas
- 2 tablespoons olive oil
- 1 small onion, finely chopped
- 2 cloves garlic, minced
- 1/4 cup fresh mint leaves, chopped
- Salt and pepper, to taste
- 1 tablespoon lemon juice

Fried Marinated Zucchini with Basil and Vinegar

🕐 15 mins   🍲 10 min   👤 4

O1 Heat 2 tbsp olive oil in a skillet over medium heat. Sauté sliced zucchini for 5-7 minutes until tender and golden. Remove from heat and let cool.

O2 Whisk remaining olive oil, red wine vinegar, minced garlic, salt, black pepper, and red pepper flakes (if using) in a small bowl. Combine sautéed zucchini and dressing in a large bowl, tossing well to coat.

O3 Add chopped basil leaves and toss gently. Serve immediately or refrigerate for 30 minutes to allow flavors to meld.

NUTRITIONAL VALUE

110 calories, 2g protein, 6g carbohydrates, 9g fat, 2g fiber, 0mg cholesterol, 100mg sodium, 300mg potassium.

INGREDIENTS

- 4 medium zucchinis, thinly sliced
- 1/4 cup olive oil
- 2 tablespoons red wine vinegar
- 1 clove garlic, minced
- 1/4 cup fresh basil leaves, chopped
- Salt and black pepper, to taste
- 1/4 teaspoon red pepper flakes (optional)

INGREDIENTS

- 1 medium butternut squash, peeled and diced, 2 tbsp olive oil
- 1 small red onion, finely chopped
- 2 cloves garlic, minced
- 1 cup diced tomatoes, salt and pepper
- 1/2 cup green olives, pitted and chopped, 2 tbsp capers, rinsed
- 2 tablespoons red wine vinegar
- 1 tablespoon honey (optional)
- 1/4 cup fresh parsley, chopped

Corsican Butternut Squash Caponata

 15 mins 30 min 4

01 Preheat oven to 400°F (200°C). Toss diced butternut squash with olive oil, salt, and pepper. Roast for 20-25 minutes until tender and caramelized.

02 In a skillet, heat olive oil over medium heat. Sauté red onion and garlic for 5 minutes until softened. Stir in diced tomatoes, olives, capers, red wine vinegar, and honey (if using). Cook for 5 minutes until combined and heated through.

03 Add roasted butternut squash to skillet and mix gently. Cook for 2-3 minutes to meld flavors. Remove from heat, sprinkle with fresh parsley, and serve warm.

NUTRITIONAL VALUE

150 calories, 2g protein, 18g carbohydrates, 9g fat, 4g fiber, 0mg cholesterol, 320mg sodium, 450mg potassium.

INGREDIENTS

- 2 large red bell peppers, roasted and peeled, 1 cup walnuts, toasted
- 1/4 cup olive oil
- 2 tbsp lemon juice, 2 tbsp tomato paste, 1 tbsp pomegranate molasses
- 1 tsp cumin, 1/2 tsp smoked paprika
- 1/4 teaspoon cayenne pepper
- Salt and black pepper, to taste

Lebanese Muhammara

 15 mins 10 min 4

01 Preheat oven to 400°F (200°C). Roast red bell peppers for 10 minutes until charred and tender. Peel and set aside.

02 In a food processor, combine roasted peppers, toasted walnuts, olive oil, lemon juice, tomato paste, pomegranate molasses, cumin, smoked paprika, cayenne, salt, and pepper. Blend until smooth and creamy.

03 Transfer to a serving bowl and drizzle with extra olive oil if desired. Serve immediately or refrigerate for 30 minutes to let flavors meld.

NUTRITIONAL VALUE

180 calories, 4g protein, 6g carbohydrates, 15g fat, 3g fiber, 0mg cholesterol, 150mg sodium, 250mg potassium.

SNACKS

INGREDIENTS

- ·8 oz feta cheese, cut into cubes
- I cup Kalamata olives, pitted
- I cup cherry tomatoes
- 1/4 cup olive oil, 2 tbsp fresh oregano, chopped, I tbsp lemon juice
- Salt and black pepper, to taste
- Skewers

Greek Feta and Olive Keto Skewers

 10 mins 0 min 4

O1 In a bowl, whisk together olive oil, fresh oregano, lemon juice, salt, and black pepper.

O2 Thread feta cheese cubes, Kalamata olives, and cherry tomatoes onto skewers, alternating as desired. Place skewers on a serving platter and drizzle with the olive oil mixture.

O3 Let marinate for at least 10 minutes before serving to allow flavors to meld. Serve immediately.

NUTRITIONAL VALUE	200 calories, 6g protein, 5g carbohydrates, 18g fat, 2g fiber, 25mg cholesterol, 350mg sodium, 150mg potassium.

INGREDIENTS

- I can (5 oz) tuna in olive oil, drained
- 2 tablespoons capers, rinsed and chopped, I red onion, finely chopped
- I clove garlic, minced, salt, pepper
- 2 tbsp fresh lemon juice
- 1/4 cup fresh parsley, chopped
- 2 tbsp olive oil, 4 slices of keto-friendly bread, toasted

Maltese Tuna and Caper Bruschetta

 10 mins 5 min 4

O1 In a medium bowl, combine drained tuna, capers, red onion, garlic, lemon juice, parsley, and olive oil. Mix well and season with salt and pepper.

O2 Toast the slices of keto-friendly bread until golden brown.

O3 Spoon the tuna mixture evenly over the toasted bread slices. Serve immediately, garnished with additional parsley if desired.

NUTRITIONAL VALUE	200 calories, 15g protein, 4g carbohydrates, 14g fat, 1g fiber, 30mg cholesterol, 350mg sodium, 200mg potassium.

Stuffed Mini Peppers with Cream Cheese

🕐 15 mins   🍲 0 min   👤 4

01   Slice the tops off the mini bell peppers and remove the seeds.

02   In a medium bowl, mix softened cream cheese, crumbled feta, cumin, smoked paprika, garlic powder, cayenne (if using), fresh dill, salt, and black pepper until well combined. Stuff each mini bell pepper with the mixture.

03   Arrange stuffed peppers on a serving platter. Serve immediately or refrigerate until ready to serve.

INGREDIENTS

- 12 mini bell peppers
- 8 oz cream cheese, softened
- 1/4 cup feta cheese, crumbled
- I tsp cumin, smoked paprika
- 1/2 teaspoon garlic powder
- 1/4 teaspoon cayenne pepper
- 2 tablespoons fresh dill, chopped
- Salt and black pepper, to taste

NUTRITIONAL VALUE   180 calories, 4g protein, 6g carbohydrates, 15g fat, 2g fiber, 40mg cholesterol, 300mg sodium, 200mg potassium.

Lebanese Za'atar Spiced Pecans

🕐 10 mins   🍲 15 min   👤 4

01   Preheat the oven to 350°F (175°C).

02   In a large bowl, combine pecan halves, olive oil, za'atar, cumin, smoked paprika, salt, and black pepper. Toss to coat evenly. Spread spiced pecans in a single layer on a parchment-lined baking sheet.

03   Bake for 15 minutes, stirring halfway through, until toasted and fragrant. Allow to cool before serving.

INGREDIENTS

- 2 cups pecan halves
- 2 tablespoons olive oil
- 2 tablespoons za'atar spice blend
- I teaspoon ground cumin
- 1/2 teaspoon smoked paprika
- Salt and black pepper, to taste

NUTRITIONAL VALUE   210 calories, 3g protein, 5g carbohydrates, 20g fat, 3g fiber, 0mg cholesterol, 80mg sodium, 120mg potassium.

INGREDIENTS

- 2 large eggplants
- 1/4 cup tahini, 2 tbsp lemon juice
- 2 cloves garlic, minced
- 1/4 cup olive oil, divided
- Salt and black pepper, 1 tsp cumin
- 1/4 cup fresh parsley, chopped
- 4 low-carb pita bread, cut into triangles

Egyptian Baba Ganoush with Keto Pita Chips

🕐 15 mins   🍲 30 min   👤 4

O1   Preheat oven to 400°F (200°C). Prick eggplants and roast for 30 minutes, turning occasionally. Allow to cool.

O2   Peel eggplants and blend flesh with tahini, lemon juice, garlic, 2 tbsp olive oil, salt, pepper, and cumin until smooth. Transfer to a bowl, drizzle with remaining olive oil, and sprinkle with parsley.

O3   Preheat oven to 350°F (175°C). Brush pita triangles with olive oil and bake for 10-12 minutes until crispy. Serve baba ganoush with pita chips.

NUTRITIONAL VALUE   250 calories, 5g protein, 8g carbohydrates, 22g fat, 4g fiber, 0mg cholesterol, 180mg sodium, 350mg potassium.

INGREDIENTS

- 2 large eggplants
- 2 tablespoons olive oil
- 1 teaspoon sea salt
- 1/2 teaspoon black pepper
- 1 teaspoon dried oregano

Sicilian Eggplant Chips with Sea Salt

🕐 25 mins   🍲 10 min   👤 4

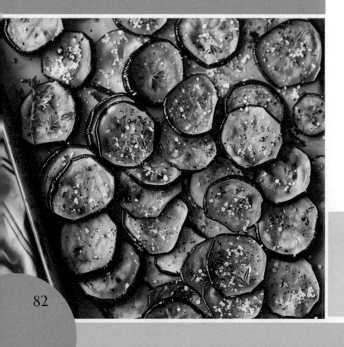

O1   Preheat the oven to 375°F (190°C). Line a baking sheet with parchment paper.

O2   Slice eggplants into 1/8 inch rounds. Toss with olive oil, sea salt, black pepper, and dried oregano in a large bowl until evenly coated.

O3   Arrange slices in a single layer on the baking sheet. Bake for 20-25 minutes, flipping halfway, until crispy and golden brown. Allow to cool slightly before serving.

NUTRITIONAL VALUE   90 calories, 1g protein, 7g carbohydrates, 7g fat, 3g fiber, 0mg cholesterol, 150mg sodium, 250mg potassium.

Cypriot Halloumi Fries with Lemon Yogurt Dip

🕐 10 mins   🍲 15 min   👤 4

INGREDIENTS

- 8 oz halloumi cheese
- 2 tablespoons olive oil
- 1/2 cup Greek yogurt
- 1 tablespoon lemon juice
- 1 teaspoon lemon zest
- 1 tablespoon fresh dill, chopped
- Salt and black pepper, to taste

O1 Cut halloumi cheese into fry-shaped sticks.

O2 Heat olive oil in a skillet over medium-high heat. Cook halloumi sticks for 2-3 minutes on each side until golden brown and crispy. Drain on paper towels.

O3 Mix Greek yogurt, lemon juice, lemon zest, fresh dill, salt, and black pepper in a small bowl. Serve halloumi fries hot with the lemon yogurt dip on the side.

NUTRITIONAL VALUE

250 calories, 14g protein, 4g carbohydrates, 20g fat, 0g fiber, 50mg cholesterol, 800mg sodium, 50mg potassium.

Israeli Avocado and Tahini Dip

🕐 10 mins   🍲 0 min   👤 4

INGREDIENTS

- 2 ripe avocados, peeled and pitted
- 1/4 cup tahini
- 2 tablespoons lemon juice
- 1 clove garlic, minced
- 1/4 cup fresh cilantro, chopped
- 2 tablespoons olive oil
- Salt and black pepper, to taste
- 1/4 teaspoon ground cumin

O1 Mash avocados in a medium bowl until smooth.

O2 Add tahini, lemon juice, minced garlic, chopped cilantro, olive oil, salt, black pepper, and ground cumin. Mix until well combined and adjust seasoning to taste.

O3 Transfer dip to a serving bowl. Serve immediately with keto-friendly chips or vegetable sticks.

NUTRITIONAL VALUE

210 calories, 3g protein, 8g carbohydrates, 19g fat, 6g fiber, 0mg cholesterol, 150mg sodium, 450mg potassium.

INGREDIENTS

- 2 large cucumbers
- I cup Greek yogurt
- I tablespoon lemon juice
- I clove garlic, minced
- I tablespoon fresh dill, chopped
- I tablespoon fresh mint, chopped
- Salt and black pepper, to taste
- I tablespoon olive oil

Greek Tzaïziki Cucumber Cups

🕐 15 mins   🍲 0 min   👤 4

O1   Slice cucumbers into I-inch rounds and scoop out the centers to create cups.

O2   In a medium bowl, mix Greek yogurt, lemon juice, minced garlic, chopped dill, chopped mint, salt, and black pepper until well combined. Spoon the tzatziki mixture into the cucumber cups.

O3   Drizzle with olive oil and serve immediately as a refreshing appetizer or snack.

NUTRITIONAL VALUE

90 calories, 4g protein, 5g carbohydrates, 6g fat, 1g fiber, 5mg cholesterol, 50mg sodium, 200mg potassium.

INGREDIENTS

- I large cucumber, sliced into rounds
- 1/2 lb shrimp, peeled and deveined
- I tbsp olive oil, I clove garlic, minced
- I tablespoon lemon juice
- I tsp lemon zest, I tbsp dill, chopped
- 4 oz cream cheese, softened
- Salt and pepper, to taste

Adriaïic Shrimp and Cucumber Canapés

🕐 20 mins   🍲 5 min   👤 4

O1   Heat olive oil in a skillet over medium heat. Add garlic and shrimp, cooking until shrimp are pink and cooked through, about 3-4 minutes. Remove from heat and toss shrimp with lemon juice, lemon zest, and chopped dill. Season with salt and pepper.

O2   Spread a small amount of cream cheese on each cucumber round. Place a shrimp on top of the cream cheese on each cucumber round.

O3   Arrange on a platter and serve immediately.

NUTRITIONAL VALUE

160 calories, 16g protein, 4g carbohydrates, 9g fat, 1g fiber, 85mg cholesterol, 220mg sodium, 200mg potassium.

Moroccan Spiced Roast Almonds

 5 mins 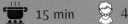 15 min 4

INGREDIENTS

- 2 cups raw almonds
- 2 tablespoons olive oil
- 1 tsp ground cumin, paprika
- 1/2 teaspoon ground cinnamon
- 1/2 teaspoon ground coriander
- 1/2 teaspoon ground ginger
- 1/4 teaspoon cayenne pepper (optional), salt, to taste

01 Preheat the oven to 350°F (175°C).

02 Toss almonds with olive oil, cumin, paprika, cinnamon, coriander, ginger, cayenne (if using), and salt until evenly coated. Spread in a single layer on a baking sheet.

03 Roast for 15 minutes, stirring halfway, until golden brown and fragrant. Cool before serving or storing in an airtight container.

NUTRITIONAL VALUE

210 calories, 6g protein, 8g carbohydrates, 18g fat, 4g fiber, 0mg cholesterol, 150mg sodium, 250mg potassium.

Labneh Balls with Herbs and Olive Oil

 10 mins 0 min 4

INGREDIENTS

- 1 cup labneh (strained yogurt)
- 2 tablespoons fresh herbs (such as parsley, dill, or mint), chopped
- 2 tablespoons extra virgin olive oil
- Salt, to taste
- Black pepper, to taste

01 In a mixing bowl, combine labneh and chopped herbs. Season with salt and black pepper to taste.

02 Mix well until herbs are evenly distributed. Roll small portions of the mixture into balls using your hands.

03 Arrange the labneh balls on a serving plate and drizzle with extra virgin olive oil just before serving.

NUTRITIONAL VALUE

90 calories, 5g protein, 2g carbohydrates, 7g fat, 0g fiber, 5mg cholesterol, 20mg sodium, 120mg potassium.

INGREDIENTS

- 2 large fennel bulbs, trimmed and sliced, 2 tablespoons olive oil
- 1 lemon, juiced and zested
- 2 cloves garlic, minced
- 1 teaspoon dried thyme
- Salt and pepper, to taste
- Fresh parsley, chopped (for garnish)

Roasted Fennel with Lemon and Herbs

🕐 10 mins   🍲 25 min   👤 4

O1   Preheat your oven to 400°F (200°C).

O2   In a large bowl, toss sliced fennel with olive oil, lemon juice, lemon zest, minced garlic, dried thyme, salt, and pepper until evenly coated. Spread in a single layer on a baking sheet.

O3   Roast for 20-25 minutes, stirring halfway, until tender and caramelized. Transfer to a serving dish and garnish with fresh parsley before serving.

NUTRITIONAL VALUE

90 calories, 1g protein, 8g carbohydrates, 7g fat, 3g fiber, 0mg cholesterol, 85mg sodium, 480mg potassium.

INGREDIENTS

- 8 oz feta cheese, cut into cubes
- 1/4 cup olive oil
- 2 tbsp fresh lemon juice, 1 tbsp lemon zest, salt and pepper, to taste
- 2 tablespoons fresh mint, chopped
- 1 garlic clove, minced

Corsican Mint and Lemon Marinated Feta

🕐 10 mins   🍲 0 min   👤 4

O1   In a bowl, whisk together olive oil, lemon juice, lemon zest, chopped mint, and minced garlic.

O2   Add the cubed feta cheese and gently toss to coat. Season with salt and pepper.

O3   Cover and marinate in the refrigerator for at least 2 hours. Serve chilled as a snack or appetizer.

NUTRITIONAL VALUE

200 calories, 5g protein, 1g carbohydrates, 19g fat, 0g fiber, 25mg cholesterol, 400mg sodium, 40mg potassium.

Greek Cauliflower Fritters with Dill

 15 mins 15 min 👤 4

INGREDIENTS

- 1 small head cauliflower, grated
- 2 eggs
- 1/4 cup almond flour
- 1/4 cup crumbled feta cheese
- 2 tablespoons chopped fresh dill
- Salt and pepper to taste
- Olive oil for frying

01 In a large bowl, combine grated cauliflower, eggs, almond flour, feta cheese, chopped dill, salt, and pepper. Mix until well combined.

02 Heat olive oil in a skillet over medium heat. Scoop about 2 tablespoons of the cauliflower mixture and shape it into small patties.

03 Cook the patties in the skillet for 3-4 minutes on each side, or until golden brown. Remove and place on a paper towel-lined plate to drain excess oil. Serve hot.

NUTRITIONAL VALUE

120 calories, 6g protein, 5g carbohydrates, 8g fat, 2g fiber, 60mg cholesterol, 200mg sodium, 300mg potassium.

Sicilian Anchovy and Olive Tapenade

 10 mins 0 min 👤 4

INGREDIENTS

- 1 cup pitted black olives
- 2 tablespoons capers
- 4 anchovy fillets
- 2 cloves garlic, minced
- 2 tablespoons fresh lemon juice
- 1/4 cup extra virgin olive oil
- Salt and pepper to taste

01 In a food processor, combine black olives, capers, anchovy fillets, minced garlic, and fresh lemon juice. Pulse until finely chopped.

02 With the processor running, slowly drizzle in extra virgin olive oil until a smooth paste forms. Season with salt and pepper to taste, and pulse to combine.

03 Transfer tapenade to a serving bowl and refrigerate until ready to serve.

NUTRITIONAL VALUE

120 calories, 1g protein, 2g carbohydrates, 12g fat, 1g fiber, 5mg cholesterol, 400mg sodium, 100mg potassium.

INGREDIENTS

- 1 cup ricotta cheese
- 2 tbsp fresh lemon juice, 1 tsp lemon zest, 2 tbsp fresh basil, chopped
- 1 tablespoon fresh mint, chopped
- 1 tablespoon fresh parsley, chopped
- 1 clove garlic, minced
- Salt and pepper, to taste
- 2 tablespoons olive oil

Sardinian Lemon and Herb Ricotta Dip

 10 mins 0 min 👤 4

01 In a medium bowl, combine ricotta cheese, lemon juice, lemon zest, basil, mint, parsley, and garlic. Mix well.

02 Season with salt and pepper, then drizzle with olive oil and stir to combine.

03 Serve immediately with keto-friendly crackers or vegetables for dipping.

NUTRITIONAL VALUE	150 calories, 6g protein, 4g carbohydrates, 12g fat, 0g fiber, 30mg cholesterol, 100mg sodium, 120mg potassium.

INGREDIENTS

- 6 large eggs
- 2 tablespoons mayonnaise
- 1 tablespoon harissa paste
- 1 teaspoon lemon juice
- 1/2 teaspoon ground cumin
- Salt and pepper to taste
- Fresh cilantro, for garnish

Moroccan Harissa Deviled Eggs

 15 mins 10 min 4

01 Place eggs in a saucepan and cover with water. Bring to a boil, then reduce heat and simmer for 10 minutes.

02 Remove eggs and place in a bowl of ice water to cool. Once cooled, peel the eggs and slice in half lengthwise, removing yolks to a separate bowl.

03 Mash yolks with a fork, then add mayonnaise, harissa paste, lemon juice, cumin, salt, and pepper. Mix until well combined. Spoon the mixture into egg white halves and garnish with fresh cilantro before serving.

NUTRITIONAL VALUE	120 calories, 7g protein, 2g carbohydrates, 9g fat, 0.5g fiber, 215mg cholesterol, 180mg sodium, 95mg potassium.

DESSERTS

INGREDIENTS

- 1 cup heavy cream
- 1/4 cup powdered erythritol (or preferred keto-friendly sweetener)
- 1/4 cup unsalted pistachios, finely ground, 1 teaspoon rose water
- 1/2 tsp vanilla extract, 1/4 tsp almond extract, additional chopped pistachios for garnish

Turkish Pistachio and Rose Water Mousse

 15 mins   0 min   4

O1 Whip heavy cream in a large mixing bowl until stiff peaks form.

O2 Gradually fold in powdered erythritol, ground pistachios, rose water, vanilla extract, and almond extract until well combined.

O3 Divide the mousse among serving glasses or bowls. Optional: garnish with chopped pistachios. Refrigerate for at least 1 hour before serving to set.

NUTRITIONAL VALUE	280 calories, 4g protein, 6g carbohydrates, 27g fat, 1g fiber, 90mg cholesterol, 20mg sodium, 120mg potassium.

INGREDIENTS

- 2 ripe avocados
- 1/2 cup fresh lime juice
- 1/4 cup water
- 1/4 cup erythritol
- 1 tablespoon lime zest
- 1/2 teaspoon vanilla extract
- Pinch of salt

Spanish Lime and Avocado Sorbet

 15 mins   0 min   4

O1 Scoop out the avocado flesh and place it in a blender.

O2 Add lime juice, water, erythritol, lime zest, vanilla extract, and a pinch of salt. Blend until smooth and creamy.

O3 Pour into a shallow dish and freeze. Every 30 minutes, stir with a fork to break up ice crystals. Repeat for 2-3 hours until the sorbet is firm but scoopable.

NUTRITIONAL VALUE	120 calories, 1g protein, 10g carbohydrates, 10g fat, 6g fiber, 0mg cholesterol, 5mg sodium, 300mg potassium.

Sicilian Orange and Almond Flour Cake

🕐 15 mins   🍲 40 min   👤 4

01 Preheat oven to 350°F (175°C). Grease a 9-inch round cake pan and line with parchment. Boil oranges for 1 hour until soft. Drain and cool.

02 Cut oranges, remove seeds, and puree. In a bowl, beat eggs and erythritol until fluffy. Add almond flour, baking powder, salt, and orange puree. Mix well.

03 Pour batter into the pan and smooth the top. Bake for 35-40 minutes until a toothpick comes out clean. Cool in the pan for 10 minutes, then transfer to a rack. Dust with powdered erythritol if desired before serving.

NUTRITIONAL VALUE

220 calories, 8g protein, 12g carbohydrates, 16g fat, 3g fiber, 120mg cholesterol, 250mg sodium, 200mg potassium.

INGREDIENTS

- 2 large oranges
- 4 eggs, 1/2 cup almond flour
- 1/2 cup erythritol (or preferred keto-friendly sweetener)
- 1 tsp baking powder
- 1/4 tsp salt
- Optional: powdered erythritol for dusting

Moroccan Spiced Chocolate Truffles

🕐 15 mins   🍲 5 min   👤 4

01 Chop dark chocolate and place in a bowl.

02 Heat heavy cream until it simmers. Pour over chocolate and let sit for 1-2 minutes, then stir until smooth. Add cinnamon, ginger, cloves, and cayenne. Stir to combine.

03 Refrigerate for 1-2 hours until firm. Scoop and roll into balls. Coat in cocoa powder. Refrigerate for another 30 minutes. Serve chilled.

INGREDIENTS

- 4 oz dark chocolate (at least 85% cocoa), 1/4 cup heavy cream
- 1/2 tsp ground cinnamon
- 1/4 tsp ground ginger
- 1/8 tsp ground cloves
- Pinch of cayenne pepper
- Unsweetened cocoa powder, for coating

NUTRITIONAL VALUE

180 calories, 2g protein, 8g carbohydrates, 16g fat, 3g fiber, 30mg cholesterol, 5mg sodium, 100mg potassium.

INGREDIENTS

- I cup unsweetened shredded coconut
- 1/2 cup almond flour
- 1/4 cup granulated erythritol
- 2 eggs, 1/4 cup melted butter
- 1/2 tsp vanilla extract
- 1/2 tsp baking powder
- Pinch of salt, slivered almonds for garnish (optional)

Egyptian Coconut and Vanilla Basbousa

 10 mins   30 min   4

O1 Preheat the oven to 350°F (175°C). Grease a small baking dish or cake pan.

O2 In a bowl, mix shredded coconut, almond flour, erythritol, eggs, melted butter, vanilla extract, baking powder, and a pinch of salt until well combined. Transfer the mixture to the prepared dish and spread evenly. Score into diamond or square shapes. Place a slivered almond in the center of each piece if desired.

O3 Bake for 25-30 minutes until golden brown and set. Cool for a few minutes before serving.

NUTRITIONAL VALUE	280 calories, 6g protein, 7g carbohydrates, 26g fat, 4g fiber, 110mg cholesterol, 250mg sodium, 180mg potassium.

INGREDIENTS

- 1/2 cup granulated erythritol
- 1/4 cup water
- I cup heavy cream
- I cup unsweetened almond milk
- 4 large eggs
- I tsp almond extract
- 1/4 cup finely ground almond flour

Spanish Almond Flan

 10 mins   45 min   4

O1 Preheat oven to 350°F (175°C). Grease four ramekins. In a saucepan, combine erythritol and water over medium heat, stirring until dissolved into a light syrup. Let cool slightly.

O2 Whisk together heavy cream, almond milk, eggs, almond extract, and almond flour. Gradually pour in cooled syrup, whisking continuously.

O3 Divide mixture among ramekins. Place in a baking dish and add hot water halfway up the sides. Bake for 40-45 minutes until set but jiggly. Cool, then refrigerate for at least 2 hours. Run a knife around edges and invert to serve.

NUTRITIONAL VALUE	280 calories, 7g protein, 5g carbohydrates, 25g fat, 1g fiber, 180mg cholesterol, 90mg sodium, 150mg potassium.

Cretan Honey and Thyme Panna Cotta

🕐 10 mins   🍲 10 min   👨 4

O1 In a saucepan, heat heavy cream, almond milk, erythritol, vanilla extract, and thyme until hot but not boiling. Bloom gelatin in cold water.

O2 Remove the cream mixture from heat and stir in gelatin until dissolved. Pour into ramekins, filling each three-quarters full. Refrigerate for 4 hours until set.

O3 Before serving, drizzle with Cretan honey and optionally garnish with fresh thyme leaves.

NUTRITIONAL VALUE

240 calories, 3g protein, 3g carbohydrates, 24g fat, 0g fiber, 90mg cholesterol, 30mg sodium, 100mg potassium.

INGREDIENTS

- 1 cup heavy cream
- 1 cup unsweetened almond milk
- 1/4 cup granulated erythritol
- 1 tsp vanilla extract, 1 tsp fresh thyme leaves, 2 tsp gelatin powder
- 2 tbsp cold water
- 2 tbsp Cretan honey (or any sugarfree honey substitute)

French Lavender and Berry Tart

🕐 20 mins   🍲 15 min   👨 4

O1 Preheat your oven to 350°F (175°C) and grease a tart pan.

O2 Mix almond flour, powdered erythritol, melted butter, and dried lavender in a bowl. Press the mixture into the tart pan to form the crust. Bake for 10-12 minutes until lightly golden brown.

O3 Toss mixed berries with lemon juice and powdered erythritol. Once the crust has cooled, arrange the berries on top. Refrigerate the tart for at least 1 hour before serving.

NUTRITIONAL VALUE

280 calories, 7g protein, 9g carbohydrates, 25g fat, 4g fiber, 30mg cholesterol, 10mg sodium, 180mg potassium.

INGREDIENTS

- 1 1/2 cups almond flour
- 1/4 cup powdered erythritol
- 1/4 cup unsalted butter, melted
- 1 tsp dried culinary lavender
- 1 cup mixed berries (such as raspberries, blueberries, and strawberries), 1 tbsp lemon juice
- 1 tbsp powdered erythritol

INGREDIENTS

- 1 cup almond flour, 1/4 cup coconut flour, 2 tbsp powdered erythritol
- 1/4 tsp salt, 1 large egg
- 2 tbsp melted butter
- 1/2 cup chopped walnuts
- 2 tbsp powdered erythritol
- 1/2 tsp ground cinnamon
- 1/4 cup sugarfree maple syrup
- 1/4 cup water

Greek Baklava Rolls with Keto Phyllo

🕐 30 mins   🍲 25 min   👤 4

O1 Preheat oven to 350°F (175°C) and line a baking sheet with parchment. Combine almond flour, coconut flour, erythritol, salt, egg, and butter. Knead into dough, roll out thin, and mix walnuts, erythritol, and cinnamon.

O2 Spread walnut mix over dough. Roll into a log, slice into 8 pieces, and bake for 20-25 minutes until golden.

O3 Simmer sugar-free syrup and water for 5 minutes. Drizzle over warm rolls. Cool slightly before serving.

NUTRITIONAL VALUE

265 calories, 7g protein, 7g carbohydrates, 23g fat, 3g fiber, 40mg cholesterol, 180mg sodium, 140mg potassium.

INGREDIENTS

- 4 shots of espresso
- 4 scoops of keto friendly vanilla gelato
- 1/4 cup sugar free chocolate shavings (optional)

Italian Espresso Affogato with Keto Gelato

🕐 10 mins   🍲 5 min   👤 4

O1 Brew 4 shots of espresso using an espresso machine or moka pot.

O2 While hot, scoop keto vanilla gelato into serving glasses or bowls. Pour one shot of espresso over each scoop.

O3 Optionally, sprinkle sugar-free chocolate shavings on top. Serve immediately.

NUTRITIONAL VALUE

85 calories, 1g protein, 4g carbohydrates, 7g fat, 1g fiber, 15mg cholesterol, 5mg sodium, 50mg potassium.

Turkish Delight Style Gelatin Bites (SugarFree)

 10 mins 5 min 4

INGREDIENTS

- 2 cups water
- 2 tablespoons gelatin powder
- 1/4 cup powdered erythritol
- 1 teaspoon rose water
- 1/4 cup chopped pistachios
- 1/4 cup unsweetened shredded coconut (optional)

01 In a saucepan, sprinkle gelatin powder over water and let bloom for 5 minutes.

02 Place the saucepan over low heat and stir until the gelatin dissolves. Add powdered erythritol and rose water, stirring until combined.

03 Pour the mixture into silicone molds or a parchment-lined baking dish. Sprinkle chopped pistachios and shredded coconut (if using) on top. Refrigerate for at least 2 hours until set. Remove from molds or cut into squares if using a baking dish.

NUTRITIONAL VALUE

60 calories, 5g protein, 1g carbohydrates, 4g fat, 0g fiber, 0mg cholesterol, 15mg sodium, 20mg potassium.

French Thyme and Honey Pudding

 10 mins 10 min 4

INGREDIENTS

- 1 cup unsweetened shredded coconut, 1/2 cup almond flour
- 1/4 cup powdered erythritol
- 1/4 cup tahini
- 1/4 cup chopped pistachios
- 1 teaspoon vanilla extract
- Pinch of salt

01 In a food processor, combine black olives, capers, anchovy fillets, minced garlic, and fresh lemon juice. Pulse until finely chopped.

02 With the processor running, slowly drizzle in extra virgin olive oil until a smooth paste forms. Season with salt and pepper to taste, and pulse to combine.

03 Transfer tapenade to a serving bowl and refrigerate until ready to serve.

NUTRITIONAL VALUE

120 calories, 1g protein, 2g carbohydrates, 12g fat, 1g fiber, 5mg cholesterol, 400mg sodium, 100mg potassium.

INGREDIENTS

- 4 large eggs
- 4 oz cream cheese, softened
- 1/4 cup almond flour
- 1/4 cup chopped walnuts
- 1 tablespoon powdered erythritol
- 1 teaspoon vanilla extract
- Butter or ghee, for frying

Israeli Cheese and Walnut Blintzes

 15 mins   15 min   4

01 Beat eggs in a mixing bowl until smooth. Add cream cheese, almond flour, erythritol, and vanilla extract. Mix until smooth.

02 Heat a nonstick skillet with butter or ghee over medium heat. Pour a small amount of batter, tilt to spread thinly, and cook for 1-2 minutes per side until golden. Repeat with remaining batter.

03 Mix chopped walnuts and powdered erythritol in a separate bowl. Place a spoonful of walnut mixture on each blintz and roll up.

NUTRITIONAL VALUE	260 calories, 10g protein, 6g carbohydrates, 21g fat, 2g fiber, 195mg cholesterol, 240mg sodium, 150mg potassium.

INGREDIENTS

- 1/2 cup almond flour
- 1/4 cup powdered erythritol
- 2 large eggs, 1/2 cup heavy cream
- 1/4 teaspoon almond extract
- 1/4 teaspoon vanilla extract
- Pinch of salt
- Slivered almonds for garnish

Portuguese Almond and Egg Custard Tarts

 20 mins   25 min   4

01 Preheat oven to 350°F (175°C) and grease a muffin tin. In a bowl, combine almond flour and powdered erythritol.

02 In a separate bowl, whisk eggs, heavy cream, almond extract, vanilla extract, and salt. Pour wet ingredients into the almond flour mixture and stir until smooth.

03 Pour batter into the muffin tin, filling each cup about three-quarters full. Bake for 20-25 minutes until custards are set and lightly golden. Let cool in the tin for 5 minutes before transferring to a wire rack. Garnish with slivered almonds if desired.

NUTRITIONAL VALUE	235 calories, 7g protein, 5g carbohydrates, 21g fat, 2g fiber, 175mg cholesterol, 75mg sodium, 100mg potassium.

Maltese Lemon and Almond Biscotti

🕐 15 mins   🍲 40 min   👤 12

O1   Preheat oven to 325°F (160°C) and line a baking sheet with parchment paper. Combine almond flour, erythritol, baking powder, and lemon zest. Whisk melted butter, eggs, and vanilla. Mix wet and dry ingredients until dough forms. Fold in almonds.

O2   Shape dough into two 10x2 inch logs and place on the baking sheet. Bake for 20-25 minutes until firm and golden. Cool for 10 minutes. Reduce oven to 300°F (150°C).

O3   Slice logs into 1/2 inch slices. Bake for 15-20 minutes until golden and crisp. Cool completely before serving.

INGREDIENTS

- 1 1/2 cups almond flour
- 1/2 cup powdered erythritol
- 1 teaspoon baking powder
- Zest of 1 lemon, 1/4 cup unsalted butter, melted, 2 large eggs
- 1 teaspoon vanilla extract
- 1/4 cup chopped almonds

NUTRITIONAL VALUE

130 calories, 4g protein, 4g carbohydrates, 11g fat, 2g fiber, 50mg cholesterol, 50mg sodium, 80mg potassium.

Croatian Cherry and Cream Cheese Squares

🕐 15 mins   🍲 35 min   👤 9

O1   Preheat oven to 350°F (175°C). Grease or line an 8x8 inch baking dish. Combine almond flour, coconut flour, powdered erythritol, and salt. Stir in melted butter until crumbly. Press into the dish.

O2   Beat cream cheese and powdered erythritol until smooth. Add egg and vanilla extract, mixing well. Spread over the crust. Top with pitted sour cherries.

O3   Bake for 30-35 minutes until golden and set. Cool completely before slicing into squares.

INGREDIENTS

- 1 cup almond flour, 1/4 cup coconut flour, 1/4 cup powdered erythritol
- 1/4 tsp salt, 1/4 cup unsalted butter, melted
- 8 oz cream cheese, softened
- 1/4 cup powdered erythritol
- 1 large egg, 1 tsp vanilla extract
- 1 cup pitted sour cherries (fresh or canned), drained

NUTRITIONAL VALUE

180 calories, 5g protein, 6g carbohydrates, 15g fat, 2g fiber, 55mg cholesterol, 120mg sodium, 80mg potassium.

INGREDIENTS

- 1 1/2 cups almond flour
- 1/4 cup coconut flour, 1/4 cup erythritol, 1/2 cup butter, melted
- 2 cups ricotta cheese
- 1/4 cup erythritol
- 3 large eggs, 2 tsp bergamot zest
- 1 teaspoon vanilla extract
- 1/4 cup heavy cream

Sicilian Bergamot and Ricotta Tart

 20 mins 40 min 4

01 Preheat the oven to 350°F (175°C). Mix almond flour, coconut flour, erythritol, and melted butter. Press into a tart pan to form the crust. Bake for 10 minutes, then let cool

02 Whisk ricotta cheese, erythritol, eggs, bergamot zest, vanilla extract, and heavy cream until smooth. Pour into the cooled crust and spread evenly.

03 Bake for 30 minutes, until the filling is set and golden. Let cool before serving.

NUTRITIONAL VALUE

300 calories, 9g protein, 7g carbohydrates, 26g fat, 3g fiber, 120mg cholesterol, 180mg sodium, 80mg potassium.

INGREDIENTS

- 1 cup almond flour
- 1/2 cup granulated erythritol
- 2 tsp baking powder, 1/4 tsp salt
- 1/2 cup ricotta cheese
- 2 large eggs, 1 tsp vanilla extract
- 1/4 cup unsalted butter, melted
- Zest of 1 lemon, juice of 1 lemon

Italian Lemon Ricotta Cake (Almond Flour)

 15 mins 40 min 4

01 Preheat oven to 350°F (175°C). Grease a 6-inch cake pan and line with parchment. Mix almond flour, erythritol, baking powder, and salt.

02 Whisk ricotta, eggs, butter, lemon zest, juice, and vanilla. Combine with dry ingredients and pour into the pan.

03 Bake for 35-40 minutes until a toothpick is clean. Cool 10 minutes, then transfer to a rack. Serve with whipped cream or powdered erythritol.

NUTRITIONAL VALUE

280 calories, 10g protein, 6g carbohydrates, 24g fat, 2g fiber, 140mg cholesterol, 320mg sodium, 180mg potassium.

60-DAY MEAL PLAN

Approx. 2000 per day calories Keto Mediterranean Diet meal plan

DAY	BREAKFAST	LUNCH	SNACK	DINNER
1	Mediterranean Keto Frittata with Spinach and Feta	Adriatic Seafood Risotto, Moroccan Spiced Pumpkin and Goat Cheese Salad, Italian Lemon Ricotta Cake (Almond Flour Based)	Greek Feta and Olive Keto Skewers, Turkish Stuffed Mini Peppers with Spiced Cream Cheese	Turkish Beef Kebabs with Sumac Onions, Provençal Zucchini and Tomato Gratin, Italian Espresso Affogato with Keto Gelato
2	Sicilian Lemon Ricotta Pancakes	Moroccan Spiced Pumpkin Soup, Moroccan Roasted Carrot and Avocado Salad, French Lavender and Berry Tart (Keto Crust)	Greek Tzatziki Cucumber Cups, Maltese Tuna and Caper Bruschetta	Italian Chicken Cacciatore with Olives and Capers, Lebanese Stuffed Eggplants with Pine Nuts and Spices, Sicilian Bergamot and Ricotta Tart
3	Aegean Avocado Toast on Keto Bread	Sicilian Swordfish Steaks with Caponata, Lebanese Cauliflower Tabbouleh, Greek Baklava Rolls with Keto Phyllo	Egyptian Baba Ganoush with Keto Pita Chips, Moroccan Spiced Roast Almonds	Moroccan Lemon and Olive Chicken Tagine, Italian Lemon and Herb Roasted Mushrooms, Egyptian Coconut and Vanilla Basbousa (Keto Version)
4	Low Carb Shakshuka with Bell Peppers	Seared Tuna with Olive Tapenade Greek Village Salad with Creamy Feta Dressing, Turkish Pistachio and Rose Water Mousse	Corsican Mint and Lemon Marinated Feta, Sicilian Eggplant Chips with Sea Salt	Turkish Spiced Meatballs in Tomato and Pepper Sauce, Provençal Zucchini and Tomato Gratin, Italian Espresso Affogato with Keto Gelato
5	Caprese Omelet with Fresh Mozzarella and Basil	Keto Bouillabaisse with Saffron and Sea Bass, Andalusian Chilled Almond Soup (Ajo Blanco), Moroccan Spiced Chocolate Truffles	Turkish Stuffed Mini Peppers with Spiced Cream Cheese, Adriatic Shrimp and Cucumber Canapés	Greek Moussaka with Eggplant and Ground Lamb (Keto Version), Lebanese Lemon Garlic Cauliflower Mash, French Thyme and Honey Pudding
6	Greek Yogurt & Walnut Parfait with Cinnamon	Cretan Shrimp with Feta and Tomatoes, Tuscan Kale and Cauliflower Soup, Sicilian Orange and Almond Flour Cake	Maltese Tuna and Caper Bruschetta, Israeli Avocado and Tahini Dip	French Duck Confit with Thyme and Garlic, Greek Lemon Garlic Cauliflower Mash, Israeli Cheese and Walnut Blintzes
7	Andalusian Almond and Orange Smoothie	Italian Monkfish Piccata, Lebanese Cauliflower Tabbouleh, Cretan Honey and Thyme Panna Cotta (Sugar-Free)	Moroccan Harissa Deviled Eggs, Greek Feta and Olive Keto Skewers	Cypriot Pork Souvlaki with Lemon and Herbs, Provençal Tomato and Basil Soup, Portuguese Almond and Egg Custard Tarts (Keto Version)

8	Turkish Style Poached Eggs with Yogurt and Spiced Butter	Greek Mussels with Ouzo and Fennel, Macedonian Spinach and Feta Pie (Keto Version), Spanish Almond Flan	Corsican Mint and Lemon Marinated Feta, Greek Cauliflower Fritters with Dill	Andalusian Rabbit with Almonds and Sherry Vinegar, Lebanese Green Beans with Tomato and Garlic, Turkish Delight Style Gelatin Bites
9	Savory Olive and Tomato Galette	Moroccan Spiced Cod with Chermoula, Turkish Roasted Eggplant and Yogurt Salad, Sicilian Bergamot and Ricotta Tart	Maltese Lemon and Almond Biscotti	Portuguese Piri-Piri Grilled Chicken, Lebanese Green Beans with Tomato and Garlic, Turkish Pistachio and Rose Water Mousse
10	Catalan Spinach and Chorizo Omelette	Amalfi Lemon Butter Scallops, Mediterranean Stuffed Bell Peppers, French Lavender and Berry Tart (Keto Crust)	Greek Tzatziki Cucumber Cups	Croatian Beef Stew with Smoked Paprika, Italian Lemon and Herb Roasted Mushrooms, Maltese Rabbit and Vegetable Broth
11	Andalusian Almond and Orange Smoothie	Sicilian Cauliflower and Almond Casserole, Greek Lemon Chicken Soup (Avgolemono), Italian Lemon Ricotta Cake (Almond Flour Based)	Lebanese Za'atar Spiced Pecans, Sicilian Anchovy and Olive Tapenade	Turkish Seafood Güveç (Clay Pot Stew), Italian Lemon and Herb Roasted Mushrooms, Greek Baklava Rolls with Keto Phyllo
12	Halloumi and Asparagus Keto Skillet	Catalan Shrimp with Garlic and Parsley, Venetian Asparagus and Egg Salad, Moroccan Spiced Chocolate Truffles	Maltese Tuna and Caper Bruschetta, Moroccan Spiced Roast Almonds	Sicilian Pork Roulade with Pine Nuts and Raisins, Lebanese Lemon Garlic Cauliflower Mash, Cretan Honey and Thyme Panna Cotta (Sugar-Free)
13	Provençal Mushroom and Herb Bake	Moroccan Spiced Cod with Chermoula, Lebanese Cauliflower Tabbouleh, French Thyme and Honey Pudding	Greek Feta and Olive Keto Skewers, Corsican Mint and Lemon Marinated Feta	Italian Chicken Cacciatore with Olives and Capers, Turkish Spiced Spinach with Yogurt, Israeli Cheese and Walnut Blintzes (Keto Version)
14	Andalusian Almond and Orange Smoothie	Greek Sea Bream with Oregano and Lemon Butter, Greek Octopus Salad with Olive Oil and Lemon, Egyptian Coconut and Vanilla Basbousa	Sicilian Eggplant Chips with Sea Salt, Greek Cauliflower Fritters with Dill	Turkish Beef Kebabs with Sumac Onions, Venetian Creamy Polenta with Roasted Mushrooms, Italian Espresso Affogato with Keto Gelato
15	Moroccan Spiced Keto Porridge	Venetian Spicy Mussels in Tomato Broth, Macedonian Eggplant and Tomato Soup, Sicilian Orange and Almond Flour Cake	Egyptian Spiced Beetroot Dip, Lebanese Labneh Balls with Herbs and Olive Oil	Cypriot Halloumi and Prawn Skewers, Moroccan Cinnamon Roasted Carrots, Spanish Lime and Avocado Sorbet

16	Sicilian Lemon Ricotta Pancakes	Greek Octopus Salad with Olive Oil and Lemon, Greek Village Salad with Creamy Feta Dressing, Moroccan Spiced Chocolate Truffles	Turkish Roasted Chickpeas with Sumac, Israeli Avocado and Tahini Dip	Greek Lamb Koftas with Tzatziki Sauce, Greek Zucchini Noodles with Feta and Sundried Tomatoes, Dessert: Portuguese Almond and Egg Custard Tarts (Keto Version)
17	Mediterranean Keto Frittata with Spinach and Feta	Seared Tuna with Olive Tapenade, Lebanese Lemon Garlic Cauliflower Mash, Greek Baklava Rolls with Keto Phyllo	Turkish Stuffed Mini Peppers with Spiced Cream Cheese, Greek Tzatziki Cucumber Cups	Andalusian Rabbit with Almonds and Sherry Vinegar, Lebanese Green Beans with Tomato and Garlic, Turkish Pistachio and Rose Water Mousse
18	Greek Yogurt & Walnut Parfait with Cinnamon	Cretan Shrimp with Feta and Tomatoes, Moroccan Spiced Pumpkin and Goat Cheese Salad, Spanish Almond Flan	Corsican Butternut Squash Caponata	French Duck Confit with Thyme and Garlic, Turkish Spiced Spinach with Yogurt, Sicilian Bergamot and Ricotta Tart
19	Caprese Omelet with Fresh Mozzarella and Basil	Moroccan Spiced Pumpkin Soup, Greek Sea Bream with Oregano and Lemon Butter, Cretan Honey and Thyme Panna Cotta (Sugar-Free)	Lebanese Muhammara (Red Pepper and Walnut Spread)	Turkish Spiced Meatballs in Tomato and Pepper Sauce, Greek Zucchini Noodles with Feta and Sundried Tomatoes, Israeli Cheese and Walnut Blintzes (Keto Version)
20	Mediterranean Keto Frittata with Spinach and Feta	Catalan Beef and Mushroom Broth, Spanish Chorizo and Manchego Stuffed Peppers, Italian Lemon Ricotta Cake	Greek Cauliflower Fritters with Dill	Turkish Beef Kebabs with Sumac Onions, Portuguese Chorizo Roasted Brussels Sprouts, French Lavender and Berry Tart (Keto Crust)
21	Florentine Artichoke and Egg Cups	Greek Mussels with Ouzo and Fennel, Italian Chicken Cacciatore with Olives and Capers, Egyptian Coconut and Vanilla Basbousa	Turkish Roasted Fennel with Lemon and Herbs, Sicilian Anchovy and Olive Tapenade	Cypriot Pork Souvlaki with Lemon and Herbs, Lebanese Lemon Garlic Cauliflower Mash, Turkish Delight Style Gelatin Bites (Sugar-Free)
22	Provençal Mushroom and Herb Bake	Moroccan Spiced Cod with Chermoula, Greek Lemon Chicken Soup (Avgolemono), Sicilian Orange and Almond Flour Cake	Maltese Tuna and Caper Bruschetta, Turkish Spiced Mini Peppers with Cream Cheese	Italian Chicken Cacciatore with Olives and Capers, Provençal Tomato and Basil Soup, French Thyme and Honey Pudding
23	Portuguese Almond and Egg Custard Tarts	Venetian Creamy Polenta with Roasted Mushrooms, Greek Octopus Salad with Olive Oil and Lemon, Sicilian Bergamot and Ricotta Tart	Greek Feta and Olive Keto Skewers	French Duck Confit with Thyme and Garlic, Turkish Spiced Spinach with Yogurt, Spanish Lime and Avocado Sorbet

24	Andalusian Almond and Orange Smoothie	Sicilian Swordfish Steaks with Caponata, Italian Antipasto Salad with Salami and Provolone, Israeli Cheese and Walnut Blintzes (Keto Version)	Corsican Mint and Lemon Marinated Feta	Greek Moussaka with Eggplant and Ground Lamb, Lebanese Lemon Garlic Cauliflower Mash, Turkish Pistachio and Rose Water Mousse
25	Caprese Omelet with Fresh Mozzarella and Basil	Moroccan Spiced Cod with Chermoula, Greek Village Salad with Creamy Feta Dressing, French Lavender and Berry Tart (Keto Crust)	Sicilian Eggplant Chips with Sea Salt	Italian Sausage and Pepper Hash, Greek Zucchini Noodles with Feta and Sundried Tomatoes, Cretan Honey and Thyme Panna Cotta (Sugar-Free)
26	Greek Yogurt & Walnut Parfait with Cinnamon	Greek Sea Bream with Oregano and Lemon Butter, Turkish Roasted Eggplant and Yogurt Salad, Sicilian Orange and Almond Flour Cake	Maltese Lemon and Almond Biscotti Lebanese Za'atar Spiced Pecans	Moroccan Lemon and Olive Chicken Tagine, Provençal Zucchini and Tomato Gratin, Turkish Pistachio and Rose Water Mousse
27	Savory Olive and Tomato Galette	Cretan Shrimp with Feta and Tomatoes, Italian Zucchini and Pecorino Soup, French Thyme and Honey Pudding	Turkish Spiced Mini Peppers with Cream Cheese	Turkish Beef Kebabs with Sumac Onions, Greek Lemon Garlic Cauliflower Mash, Italian Lemon Ricotta Cake
28	Sicilian Lemon Ricotta Pancakes	Venetian Creamy Polenta with Roasted Mushrooms, Greek Octopus Salad with Olive Oil and Lemon, Dessert: Moroccan Spiced Chocolate Truffles	Maltese Tuna and Caper Bruschetta, Moroccan Spiced Roast Almonds	Andalusian Rabbit with Almonds and Sherry Vinegar, Portuguese Chorizo Roasted Brussels Sprouts, Israeli Cheese and Walnut Blintzes
29	Mediterranean Keto Frittata with Spinach and Feta	Amalfi Lemon Butter Scallops, Moroccan Roasted Carrot and Avocado Salad, Greek Baklava Rolls with Keto Phyllo	Greek Feta and Olive Keto Skewers	Turkish Spiced Meatballs in Tomato and Pepper Sauce, Provençal Zucchini and Tomato Gratin, Cretan Honey and Thyme Panna Cotta (Sugar-Free)
30	Catalan Spinach and Chorizo Omelette	Portuguese Caldo Verde with Keto Chorizo and Radishes, Andalusian Chilled Almond Soup (Ajo Blanco), Sicilian Orange and Almond Flour Cake	Turkish Stuffed Mini Peppers with Spiced Cream Cheese, Greek Tzatziki Cucumber Cups	Greek Moussaka with Eggplant and Ground Lamb, Italian Lemon and Herb Roasted Mushrooms, French Lavender and Berry Tart (Keto Crust)
31	Caprese Omelet with Fresh Mozzarella and Basil	Moroccan Spiced Cod with Chermoula, Venetian Radicchio and Goat Cheese Salad, French Lavender and Berry Tart (Keto Crust)	Greek Tzatziki Cucumber Cups	Italian Sausage and Pepper Hash, Greek Zucchini Noodles with Feta and Sundried Tomatoes, Cretan Honey and Thyme Panna Cotta (Sugar-Free)

32	Sicilian Lemon Ricotta Pancakes	Venetian Creamy Polenta with Roasted Mushrooms, Greek Octopus Salad with Olive Oil and Lemon, Dessert: Moroccan Spiced Chocolate Truffles	Maltese Tuna and Caper Bruschetta, Moroccan Spiced Roast Almonds	Andalusian Rabbit with Almonds and Sherry Vinegar, Portuguese Chorizo Roasted Brussels Sprouts, Israeli Cheese and Walnut Blintzes
33	Provençal Mushroom and Herb Bake	Greek Sea Bream with Oregano and Lemon Butter, Turkish Spinach and Yogurt Soup, Egyptian Coconut and Vanilla Basbousa	Lebanese Muhammara (Red Pepper and Walnut Spread)	Moroccan Lemon and Olive Chicken Tagine, Provençal Zucchini and Tomato Gratin, Turkish Pistachio and Rose Water Mousse
34	Florentine Artichoke and Egg Cups	Greek Mussels with Ouzo and Fennel, Mediterranean Stuffed Bell Peppers, Dessert: Italian Lemon Ricotta Cake	Maltese Tuna and Caper Bruschetta, Moroccan Spiced Roast Almonds	Turkish Spiced Meatballs in Tomato and Pepper Sauce, Lebanese Lemon Garlic Cauliflower Mash, French Thyme and Honey Pudding
35	Aegean Avocado Toast on Keto Bread	Adriatic Seafood Risotto, Greek Spinach and Strawberry Salad with Walnuts, French Lavender and Berry Tart	Egyptian Baba Ganoush with Keto Pita Chips, Greek Tzatziki Cucumber Cups	Greek Lamb Koftas with Tzatziki Sauce, Moroccan Cinnamon Roasted Carrots, Italian Espresso Affogato with Keto Gelato
36	Moroccan Spiced Keto Porridge	Cypriot Halloumi and Prawn Skewers, Andalusian Chilled Almond Soup (Ajo Blanco), Dessert: Spanish Lime and Avocado Sorbet	Turkish Stuffed Mini Peppers with Spiced Cream Cheese, Corsican Mint and Lemon Marinated Feta	Turkish Beef Kebabs with Sumac Onions, Lebanese Cauliflower Tabbouleh, Moroccan Spiced Chocolate Truffles
37	Caprese Omelet with Fresh Mozzarella and Basil	Amalfi Lemon Butter Scallops, Portuguese Kale and Almond Soup, Greek Baklava Rolls with Keto Phyllo	Moroccan Spiced Roast Almonds	Andalusian Rabbit with Almonds and Sherry Vinegar, Provençal Zucchini and Tomato Gratin, Cretan Honey and Thyme Panna Cotta
38	Turkish Style Poached Eggs with Yogurt and Spiced Butter	Cretan Shrimp with Feta and Tomatoes, Moroccan Roasted Carrot and Avocado Salad, Sicilian Bergamot and Ricotta Tart	Lebanese Za'atar Spiced Pecans	Moroccan Lemon and Olive Chicken Tagine, Greek Lemon Garlic Cauliflower Mash, Spanish Almond Flan
39	Sicilian Lemon Ricotta Pancakes	Greek Octopus Salad with Olive Oil and Lemon, Andalusian Chilled Almond Soup, Egyptian Coconut and Vanilla Basbousa (Keto Version)	Lebanese Muhammara (Red Pepper and Walnut Spread)	Italian Chicken Cacciatore with Olives and Capers, Provençal Tomato and Basil Soup, French Thyme and Honey Pudding

40	Catalan Spinach and Chorizo Omelette	Seared Tuna with Olive Tapenade, Venetian Asparagus and Egg Salad, Turkish Pistachio and Rose Water Mousse	Greek Tzatziki Cucumber Cups	Turkish Spiced Meatballs in Tomato and Pepper Sauce, Italian Lemon and Herb Roasted Mushrooms, Italian Lemon Ricotta Cake
41	Florentine Artichoke and Egg Cups	Sicilian Swordfish Steaks with Caponata, Portuguese Kale and Almond Soup, Cretan Honey and Thyme Panna Cotta (Sugar-Free)	Maltese Lemon and Almond Biscotti	Andalusian Rabbit with Almonds and Sherry Vinegar, Lebanese Lemon Garlic Cauliflower Mash, French Thyme and Honey Pudding
42	Mediterranean Keto Frittata with Spinach and Feta	Greek Mussels with Ouzo and Fennel, Italian Portobello Mushrooms with Pesto, French Lavender and Berry Tart	Turkish Stuffed Mini Peppers with Spiced Cream Cheese	Greek Moussaka with Eggplant and Ground Lamb (Keto Version), Moroccan Cinnamon Roasted Carrots, Spanish Almond Flan
43	Low Carb Shakshuka with Bell Peppers	Amalfi Lemon Butter Scallops, Mediterranean Stuffed Bell Peppers, Sicilian Orange and Almond Flour Cake	Moroccan Spiced Roast Almonds, Greek Tzatziki Cucumber Cups	Turkish Beef Kebabs with Sumac Onions, Lebanese Cauliflower Tabbouleh, Italian Lemon Ricotta Cake (Almond Flour Based)
44	Andalusian Almond and Orange Smoothie	Cretan Shrimp with Feta and Tomatoes, Tuscan Kale and Cauliflower Soup, French Thyme and Honey Pudding	Lebanese Za'atar Spiced Pecans, Maltese Tuna and Caper Bruschetta	Italian Chicken Cacciatore with Olives and Capers, Portuguese Chorizo Roasted Brussels Sprouts, Turkish Pistachio and Rose Water Mousse
45	Aegean Avocado Toast on Keto Bread	Greek Octopus Salad with Olive Oil and Lemon, Moroccan Roasted Carrot and Avocado Salad, Egyptian Coconut and Vanilla Basbousa	Corsican Mint and Lemon Marinated Feta	Greek Lamb Koftas with Tzatziki Sauce, Provençal Zucchini and Tomato Gratin, Israeli Cheese and Walnut Blintzes
46	Sicilian Lemon Ricotta Pancakes	Venetian Creamy Polenta with Roasted Mushrooms, Greek Sea Bream with Oregano and Lemon Butter, Moroccan Spiced Chocolate Truffles	Egyptian Baba Ganoush with Keto Pita Chips	Turkish Spiced Meatballs in Tomato and Pepper Sauce, Lebanese Lemon Garlic Cauliflower Mash, French Lavender and Berry Tart
47	Caprese Omelet with Fresh Mozzarella and Basil	Cypriot Halloumi and Prawn Skewers, Provençal Tomato and Basil Soup, Greek Baklava Rolls with Keto Phyllo	Lebanese Muhammara (Red Pepper and Walnut Spread)	Andalusian Rabbit with Almonds and Sherry Vinegar, Italian Lemon and Herb Roasted Mushrooms, Egyptian Coconut and Vanilla Basbousa

48	Greek Yogurt & Walnut Parfait with Cinnamon	Sicilian Swordfish Steaks with Caponata, Moroccan Spiced Pumpkin Soup, Turkish Pistachio and Rose Water Mousse	Maltese Tuna and Caper Bruschetta	French Duck Confit with Thyme and Garlic, Portuguese Chorizo Roasted Brussels Sprouts
49	Aegean Avocado Toast on Keto Bread	Amalfi Lemon Butter Scallops, Lebanese Cauliflower Tabbouleh, Egyptian Coconut and Vanilla Basbousa	Corsican Mint and Lemon Marinated Feta, Greek Tzatziki Cucumber Cups	Greek Moussaka with Eggplant and Ground Lamb, Provençal Zucchini and Tomato Gratin, French Lavender and Berry Tart
50	Low Carb Shakshuka with Bell Peppers	Cretan Shrimp with Feta and Tomatoes, Tuscan Kale and Chorizo Soup, Moroccan Spiced Chocolate Truffles	Turkish Stuffed Mini Peppers with Spiced Cream Cheese, Greek Feta and Olive Keto Skewers	Italian Chicken Cacciatore with Olives and Capers, Lebanese Lemon Garlic Cauliflower Mash, Spanish Almond Flan
51	Sicilian Lemon Ricotta Pancakes	Seared Tuna with Olive Tapenade, Moroccan Roasted Carrot and Avocado Salad, Cretan Honey and Thyme Panna Cotta (Sugar-Free)	Greek Tzatziki Cucumber Cups	Andalusian Rabbit with Almonds and Sherry Vinegar, Provençal Zucchini and Tomato Gratin, French Lavender and Berry Tart
52	Mediterranean Keto Frittata with Spinach and Feta	Greek Octopus Salad with Olive Oil and Lemon, Venetian Creamy Polenta with Roasted Mushrooms, Sicilian Orange and Almond Flour Cake	Greek Feta and Olive Keto Skewers	Moroccan Lemon and Olive Chicken Tagine, Lebanese Lemon Garlic Cauliflower Mash, Israeli Cheese and Walnut Blintzes
53	Andalusian Almond and Orange Smoothie	Greek Sea Bream with Oregano and Lemon Butter, Italian Zucchini and Pecorino Soup, Moroccan Spiced Chocolate Truffles	Corsican Mint and Lemon Marinated Feta, Sicilian Eggplant Chips with Sea Salt	Turkish Spiced Meatballs in Tomato and Pepper Sauce, Moroccan Cinnamon Roasted Carrots, Turkish Pistachio and Rose Water Mousse
54	Greek Yogurt & Walnut Parfait with Cinnamon	Cypriot Halloumi and Prawn Skewers, Portuguese Kale and Almond Soup, French Thyme and Honey Pudding	Greek Tzatziki Cucumber Cups	Greek Lamb Koftas with Tzatziki Sauce, Provençal Zucchini and Tomato Gratin, Spanish Almond Flan
55	Aegean Avocado Toast on Keto Bread	Cretan Shrimp with Feta and Tomatoes, Lebanese Cauliflower Tabbouleh, Egyptian Coconut and Vanilla Basbousa	Maltese Tuna and Caper Bruschetta	Andalusian Rabbit with Almonds and Sherry Vinegar, Lebanese Lemon Garlic Cauliflower Mash, Italian Lemon Ricotta Cake

56	Caprese Omelet with Fresh Mozzarella and Basil	Amalfi Lemon Butter Scallops, Moroccan Roasted Carrot and Avocado Salad, Greek Baklava Rolls with Keto Phyllo	Turkish Stuffed Mini Peppers with Spiced Cream Cheese	Turkish Spiced Meatballs in Tomato and Pepper Sauce, Provençal Zucchini and Tomato Gratin, French Lavender and Berry Tart
57	Sicilian Lemon Ricotta Pancakes	Greek Mussels with Ouzo and Fennel, Portuguese Kale and Almond Soup, Italian Lemon Ricotta Cake	Egyptian Baba Ganoush with Keto Pita Chips, Moroccan Spiced Roast Almonds	Greek Moussaka with Eggplant and Ground Lamb, Lebanese Lemon Garlic Cauliflower Mash, Cretan Honey and Thyme Panna Cotta
58	Low Carb Shakshuka with Bell Peppers	Seared Tuna with Olive Tapenade, Italian Zucchini and Pecorino Soup, Moroccan Spiced Chocolate Truffles	Turkish Roasted Chickpeas with Sumac, Greek Tzatziki Cucumber Cups	Turkish Beef Kebabs with Sumac Onions, Portuguese Chorizo Roasted Brussels Sprouts, Spanish Almond Flan
59	Greek Yogurt & Walnut Parfait with Cinnamon	Sicilian Swordfish Steaks with Caponata, Greek Lemon Chicken Soup	Lebanese Muhammara (Red Pepper and Walnut Spread)	Italian Chicken Cacciatore with Olives and Capers, Provençal Zucchini and Tomato Gratin, Turkish Pistachio and Rose Water Mousse
60	Aegean Avocado Toast on Keto Bread	Cretan Shrimp with Feta and Tomatoes, Moroccan Roasted Carrot and Avocado Salad, Greek Baklava Rolls with Keto Phyllo	Maltese Lemon and Almond Biscotti	Greek Lamb Koftas with Tzatziki Sauce, Provençal Tomato and Basil Soup, Italian Lemon Ricotta Cake (Almond Flour Based)

MEASUREMENT CONVERSION CHARTS

CUP	OUNCES	MILLILITERS	TABLESPOONS
1/16 CUPS	1/2 OZ	15 ML	1 TBSP
1/8 CUPS	1 OZ	30 ML	3 TBSP
1/4 CUPS	2 OZ	59 ML	4 TBSP
1/3 CUPS	2.5 OZ	79 ML	5.5 TBSP
3/8 CUPS	3 OZ	90 ML	6 TBSP
1/2 CUPS	4 OZ	118 ML	8 TBSP
2/3 CUPS	5 OZ	158 ML	11 TBSP
3/4 CUPS	6 OZ	177 ML	12 TBSP
1 CUPS	8 OZ	240 ML	16 TBSP
2 CUPS	16 OZ	480 ML	32 TBSP
4 CUPS	32 OZ	960 ML	64 TBSP
5 CUPS	40 OZ	1180 ML	80 TBSP
6 CUPS	48 OZ	1420 ML	96 TBSP
8 CUPS	64 OZ	1895 ML	128 TBSP

MEASUREMENT

IMPERIAL	METRIC
1/2 OZ	15 G
1 OZ	29 G
2 OZ	57 G
3 OZ	85 G
4 OZ	113 G
5 OZ	141 G
6 OZ	170 G
8 OZ	227 G
10 OZ	283 G
12 OZ	340 G
13 OZ	369 G
14 OZ	397 G
15 OZ	425 G
1 LB	453 G

WEIGHT

FAHRENHEIT	CELSIUS
100 °F	37 °C
150 °F	65 °C
200 °F	93 °C
250 °F	121 °C
300 °F	150 °C
325 °F	160 °C
350 °F	180 °C
375 °F	190 °C
400 °F	200 °C
425 °F	220 °C
450 °F	230 °C
500 °F	260 °C
525 °F	274 °C
550 °F	288 °C

TEMPERATURE

Disclaimer Notice:
This book is intended to offer general information about
the Keto Mediterranean Diet and related recipes. It is
not a substitute for professional medical, nutritional, or
dietary advice. Always consult your physician, dietitian,
or another qualified health provider before starting any
new diet, particularly if you have a medical condition or
specific dietary needs. Never disregard professional
advice or delay seeking it because of something you
have read in this book. The author assumes no
responsibility for any actions taken based on the
information contained in this book.

Made in United States
Troutdale, OR
01/02/2025

27549732R00062